Barbara Learn-to-Knit Afghan Book

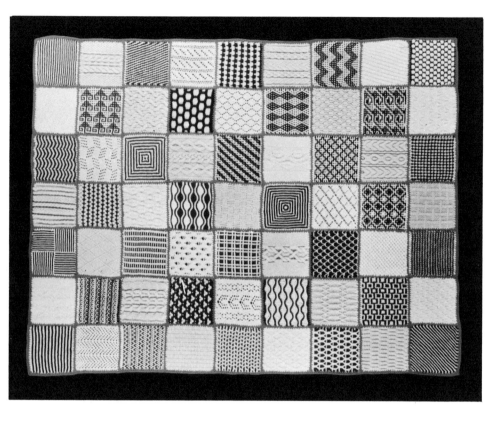

BARBARA WALKER'S
LEARN-TO-KNIT AFGHAN BOOK

by Barbara G. Walker

Photography by Werner P. Brodde
Artwork by John E. Bradley, N.J.W.S.

CHARLES SCRIBNER'S SONS / NEW YORK

1 3 5 7 9 11 13 15 17 19 MD/C 20 18 16 14 12 10 8 6 4 2
3 5 7 9 11 13 15 17 19 M/P 20 18 16 14 12 10 8 6 4 2

Printed in the United States of America
Library of Congress Catalog Card Number 73–10906
ISBN 0-684-14661-4 (cloth)
ISBN 0-684-14714-9 (paper)

CONTENTS

INTRODUCTION

This book is for all knitters, experienced and inexperienced alike. In making the Learn-To-Knit Afghan according to directions in this book, you can learn all the basic knitting skills that you are ever likely to encounter in any knitting project. Even knitters of many years' experience may find some of these skills unfamiliar, for knitting is a very big subject. It's quite possible to do a lot of knitting without ever attaining a true in-depth understanding of the mechanics of the craft.

Many knitting courses and/or instruction books teach only knitting, purling and a few increases and decreases, and then plunge into the matter of garment construction—on the assumption that all the beginner wants to do is knit endless numbers of garments in plain stockinette stitch. This book proceeds on a different assumption, i.e., that knitting anything in plain stockinette stitch is a terrible bore, and that the beginner needs to be given a chance to learn something about the really exciting part of knitting: the enormous variety of fabric designs that can be made with it.

This sampler afghan, therefore, is an inspiring project for a beginner. Each afghan square is a miniature training-ground for a new use of basic knitting techniques. No square takes so long to make that the knitter wearies of it before it is finished. And each set of instructions explains *why* a particular pattern does what it does, so the beginner is given a sound education in the fundamental principles of knitting.

The purpose of this book, then, is more than simply to teach you to knit; it is to teach you *about* knitting. Having mastered the basic skills illustrated here, neither the beginner nor the semi-skilled practitioner need be puzzled ever again by any sort of knitting directions.

The four simple processes that we might call beginner's basics—casting on, knitting, purling and binding off—are taught here according to the Continental style, which means that the working yarn is held by the left hand. Most American knitters have already learned the American style, in which the working yarn is held by the right hand. However, many of the experts switch to the Continental style eventually, because they find it is faster and easier to work. To a beginner, it makes no difference which style is learned first. Both feel equally awkward at the outset, and both become more comfortable with practice.

A good deal of nonsense has been expressed about the comparative ease of learning one style or the other in relation to right- or left-handedness. In fact, it makes no difference whether the beginning knitter is right-handed or left-handed. Knitting is a two-handed operation. The initial clumsiness experienced by the beginner is the same for everyone. Learning a different knitting style cannot cure this clumsiness; only practice can cure it. With practice, a right-handed knitter or a left-handed knitter can become equally comfortable with either style. There is also a superstition to the effect that some pattern directions can't be used in Continental style without "translating" them. This is definitely NOT true. It arises from a misunderstanding of the Continental style, or from an incorrect way of working it. Actually, pattern directions are followed in exactly the same way with either style.

Some American-style knitters wish they could switch to the Continental style, but have been unable to find a book that will teach them how to do it. If you are one of these, here's your chance. If you are a beginner, you can rest assured that learning Continental-style knitting from the ground up is a good thing, and one day you'll be glad you did it. If, on the other hand, you are an American-style knitter who wants to stay that way, you can just ignore the instructions for knitting, purling and binding off in the Beginner's Basics section, and go on to practice the techniques illustrated by the afghan patterns. All of these techniques produce the same results in either style. However, even if you're an experienced American-style knitter with no intention of switching styles, it will do you good to read the material entitled "Understanding the Knitted Fabric" in the Beginner's Basics section. A surprising number of experienced knitters are not really aware of what a knitted fabric is, or why it works as it does.

The patterns of the Learn-To-Knit Afghan are classified into eight basic groups, each group containing a variety of examples within a general type. Section by section, the afghan teaches you to use and understand Knit-Purl Combinations, Mosaic Patterns, Slip-Stitch Patterns, Twist-Stitch Patterns, Cable Patterns, Increase-and-Decrease Patterns, Lace and Special Techniques. All the techniques occurring in each general pattern type are illustrated and explained, because each example is carefully selected from among the thousands of different fabric patterns that are possible in knitting. If, after completing your Learn-To-Knit Afghan, you would like to go on learning more about other fabric patterns, you'll find large collections of them at your disposal in my other books, *A Treasury of Knitting Patterns, A Second Treasury of Knitting Patterns, Charted Knitting Designs,* and *Sampler Knitting.* Another one of my books, *Knitting From The Top,* gives detailed instructions for making knitted garments and using various types of patterns in them.

The Learn-To-Knit Afghan is an original design, intended to be useful and beautiful as well as a tangible, enduring record of your basic education in the craft of knitting. Choose your favorite colors for it, work it with pleasure and enjoy it for many years to come. It can be a teacher, a guide, an inspiration, a home decoration, a reference library for the future, a comfort on a chilly evening, a proud demonstration of your developing skill and an heirloom. How many other objects in your life can be so many worth-while things at once?

B.G.W.

Mount Kemble Lake
Morristown, New Jersey

ACKNOWLEDGMENTS

For the illustrations in this book I am profoundly grateful to two master-craftsmen, my good friends Werner P. Brodde and John E. Bradley; for materials used in the afghan, to Emile Bernat & Sons Company and the Spinnerin Yarn Company, Inc.; for general assistance, to my husband and son, Gordon N. Walker and Alan C. Walker; and for the existence of the book itself, to my editor, Elinor Parker.

Barbara Walker's
Learn-to-Knit
Afghan Book

BEGINNER'S
BASICS

CASTING ON, METHOD 1

To begin knitting, you must first put some loops, or stitches, onto one knitting needle. This is called casting on. There are at least a half-dozen good ways to do it, and at least a half-dozen more, not so good. From this book you will learn two of the best, which will serve for any purpose.

The first method of casting on begins some distance in from the free end of the yarn, leaving a long tail. The length of this free-end tail is determined by the number of stitches to be cast on. The more stitches to be cast on, the longer the tail has to be.

Hold your left hand in front of you, palm facing, and take the yarn in your right hand, leaving a tail about a yard long. Pass the *tail* strand (not the ball strand) from below between left little and ring fingers, from the palm to the back of the hand; then upward over the backs of the remaining 3 fingers, then forward (toward you) *under* the thumb, around over the top of the thumb and down across the palm to the little finger, which now curls inward to grip both strands of yarn at once (*Figure 1*).

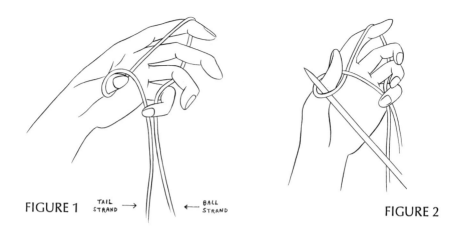

FIGURE 1   TAIL STRAND →   ← BALL STRAND   FIGURE 2

Take the needle in your right hand. Slip the needle point, from below, under the loop that faces you on the thumb (*Figure 2*). Pass the needle point from right to left *under* the strand held by the forefinger (*Figure 3*). Draw this stand toward you through the thumb loop (*Figure 4*). Drop the loop off the thumb, meanwhile putting the thumb between the 2 strands and bringing it toward you, to stretch the strands apart and tighten the loop on the needle (*Figure 5*). You have now cast on the first stitch.

FIGURE 3 AND 4

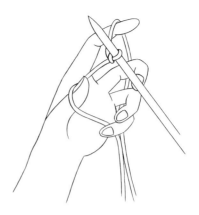

FIGURE 5—*First Stitch Cast On*

* Move the thumb over to the left, carrying the front strand of yarn on it (*Figure 6*). Again insert the needle under the strand on the thumb (*Figure 7*), then from right to left under the forefinger strand, bringing this strand toward you through the thumb loop as before. Drop the loop off the thumb and tighten the loop on the needle, as before, to make the second stitch. Repeat the whole process from * until you have used up nearly all of the free-end tail.

FIGURE 6

FIGURE 7

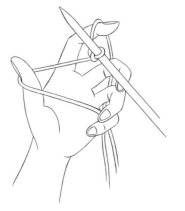

Pull the needle out of the stitches, straighten out the yarn (by pulling both ends), and start again. Keep practicing this cast-on until it comes easily and rhythmically, with an even tension. The stitches on the needle should be neat and firm, but not tight. Push them back and forth on the needle to see if they slide easily. If not, your cast-on is too tight. Keep practicing until you relax and loosen up. When you have achieved this, cast on about 30 or 35 stitches and prepare to knit.

KNITTING

After casting on the last stitch, let go of the free end of the yarn, but keep the ball strand in position between little and ring fingers and up over the backs of the fingers to the forefinger. Wrap this ball strand once more around the forefinger, under to the back, then over the finger toward you. Turn the needle around so that it points to the right, and place it in the left hand, which grips the needle with 3 fingers and thumb while the forefinger, with its yarn wraps, is held free up above. This is Knitting Position (*Figure 8*).

FIGURE 8—*Knitting Position*

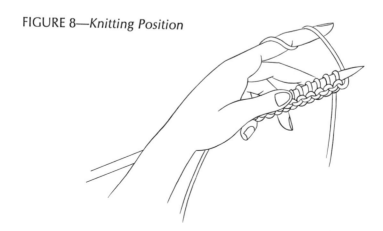

Check your Knitting Position these 4 ways: (1) The cast-on edge should lie along the bottom of the needle, with the loops *on* the needle all pointing upward. (2) The ball strand of the yarn should pass from the first stitch *behind* the needle up to the forefinger. (3) The free end of the yarn should hang downward, out of the way. (4) The hand should perch on *top* of the needle, *not* support it in the thumb joint like a pencil. In other words, the non-pointed end of the needle goes under the little finger and away from you past the outside edge of the hand. (Note: for clarity's sake, all illustrations show fingertips and stitches somewhat farther from the needle points than they really are. In practice, everything is kept quite close to the needle points.)

Take the other needle in your right hand, perching this hand on top of the needle just like the left. Look at the first loop on the left needle. This loop has one strand on the front of the needle, toward you, and the other strand on the back of the needle, away from you. * Insert the right needle point from front to back through this loop, *immediately beneath* the left needle, passing to the *left* of the front strand and to the *right* of the back strand. The needle point emerges, behind, to the *right* of the working yarn, which is held by the forefinger (*Figure 9*). Pass the needle point from right to left behind this working yarn, thus catching a loop of it, and draw this new loop through the stitch to the front (*Figure 10*). Drop the loop off the left needle. One stitch has been

FIGURE 9

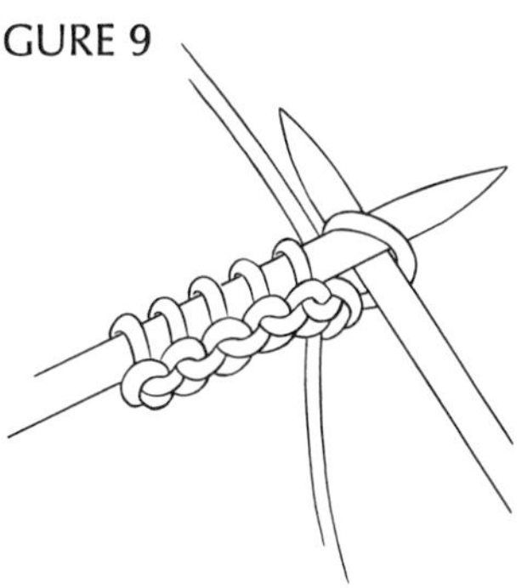

FIGURE 10

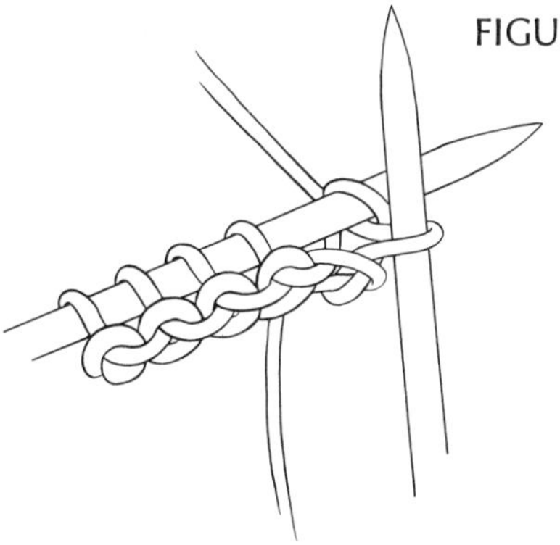

knitted and is now on the right needle. (Use the right forefinger, if needed, to hold the stitch on the right needle.) Repeat the whole process from * until you have knitted all the stitches off the left needle and onto the right needle. When the left needle is bare, you have finished your first row.

Turn. This means: turn the work around so you will be looking at the other side of it and put the needle with the stitches into the left hand, as you did after casting on. Now it becomes the left needle, and the bare needle is the right needle, ready to work the next row. Readjust your Knitting Position and work the second row just like the first. Turn again and continue knitting in the same way, row after row.

Practice, practice! Knit many rows, unravel, cast on again and knit some more. Keep practicing until you achieve a smooth, easy rhythm, and your rows look straight and tidy. Beginners invariably make their stitches either too loose or too tight, the latter being more usual. Only practice can bring you to the precise balance of tensions when the yarn slides smoothly past the grip of the little finger and the wraps over the forefinger, and you can knit evenly and closely without straining the strands between the needles or losing any of the loops off either needle.

The fabric you are making is Garter Stitch, which forms a series of horizontal ridges. You can make it in either of 2 ways: by knitting every row, or by purling every row. Purling is just backward knitting. Each stitch is formed the same way, but from behind instead of from in front. When you have come to feel more or less comfortable with knitting, cast on a new batch of 30 or 35 stitches and prepare to purl.

PURLING

After casting on the last stitch, let go of the free end of the yarn, put the needle into the left hand and wrap the yarn in Knitting Position with one exception: now the ball strand of the yarn must pass from the first stitch *not* behind the needle up to the forefinger, but *in front of* the needle up to the forefinger. This is Purling Position (*Figure 11*).

FIGURE 11—*Purling Position*

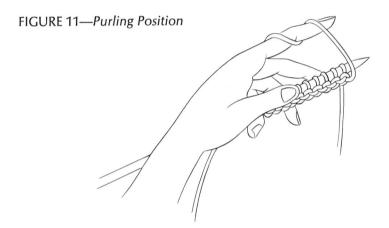

  * Insert the right needle point *from back to front* through the first loop, immediately beneath the left needle, passing to the *right* of the back strand and to the *left* of the front strand. The needle point emerges, toward you, to the *left* of the working yarn, which is held by the forefinger (*Figure 12*). With the forefinger, draw the yarn from right to left *over* the needle point to create a new loop (*Figure 13*). Take this new loop backward through the stitch to the rear (*Figure 14*). Drop the loop off the left needle. One stitch has been purled and is now on the

FIGURE 12

right needle. Repeat the whole process from *, holding the yarn always in front, the forefinger bobbing up and down, until you have purled all the stitches off the left needle and onto the right needle. Then turn and go on purling, row after row. Practice until your purled Garter Stitch looks just as neat and even as your knitted Garter Stitch.

FIGURE 13

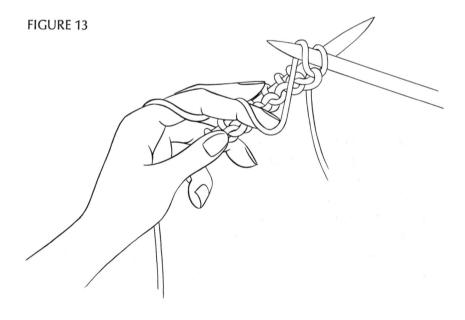

FIGURE 14

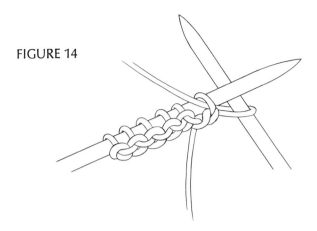

UNDERSTANDING THE KNITTED FABRIC

Now try a new fabric. Knit the first row, turn, purl the next row, turn, knit the next row, turn, purl the next row, and so on, alternating knit and purl rows. This is Stockinette Stitch, which looks very different from Garter Stitch. On the knit side, the stitches are smooth, resembling rows of little V's. On the purl side, the stitches are bumpy, resembling horizontal crescents. Garter Stitch and Stockinette Stitch are two basic knitted fabrics. When they are worked in rounds, on a circular needle, instead of in rows on straight needles, they are made in opposite ways. Stockinette Stitch is made by knitting every round. Garter Stitch is made by knitting one round and purling the next, alternately.

With a swatch of Stockinette Stitch on your needle, study the stitches themselves. You already know that each stitch has a front strand and a back strand, the front strand being on the side of the needle that you are facing, and the back strand on the other side. Notice that the front strand is *always* the *right*-hand side of the stitch, no matter whether you are looking at the knit stitches or the purl stitches. Slip a stitch off the needle, turn it so that its left-hand side is forward, and replace it on the needle. Look at it and tell yourself "Wrong, wrong." Remember it. Whenever you pick up the stitches after some unraveling, or take back to correct a mistake, always insert the needle into the stitches so their right-hand sides are toward you. Apart from incorrect picking up, the only other ways in which stitches can get into this reversed position are: incorrect purling (wrapping the yarn under the needle instead of over it); incorrect knitting; or slipping knitwise, which is not the usual way to slip but may be quite correct if directions call for it (see below).

Taking back is un-knitting (or un-purling) stitch by stitch. You do it when you want to correct a mistake that was made a few stitches previously, or when you want to undo a whole row *without* pulling out the needle and picking up all the loose stitches, risking possible loss of some of them. When several rows must be unraveled to correct a mistake a few inches down in the knitting, remove the needle, unravel to the row *above* the one with the mistake in it, slip the stitches back onto the needle and take back the final row that contains the mistake, so there will be no stitches dropped or turned the wrong way.

Practice taking back. Near the end of a row, holding yarn and needles in the usual position, un-knit (or un-purl) by inserting the left needle point into the loop *just below* the first loop on the right needle. Be sure that the right-hand side of this loop goes on the front of the left needle. Then let the loop above come off the right needle and out of the stitch that the left needle is holding. Repeat this process until you have removed the whole row from the right needle and taken it back to the left needle.

When you knit, you insert the needle through a stitch to the left of the front strand and to the right of the back strand. When you purl, you insert the needle through a stitch to the right of the back strand and to the left of the front strand. In both cases this is called working in the front loops of the stitches; it is the usual way to knit and purl. Sometimes, though, pattern directions call for working in the *back* loops of the stitches. To knit in the back loop of a stitch, you insert the needle

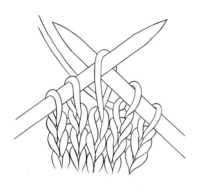

FIGURE 15—*K 1-b*   FIGURE 16—*P 1-b*

from the right, passing to the *right* of the front strand and to the *left* of the back strand (*Figure 15*). This is called "knit one in back loop," or k1-b. To purl in the back loop of a stitch, you insert the needle from the left, behind, passing to the *left* of the back strand and to the *right* of the front strand, still wrapping the yarn over the needle in front from right to left to complete the purl stitch in the usual way (*Figure 16*). This is called "purl one in back loop," or p1-b. Both of these operations result in a stitch with the strands crossed at the base of its loop.

Try this. Work some more rows of Stockinette Stitch, knitting and purling in the back loops of all the stitches. This makes Twisted Stockinette, which looks different; the vertical lines of stitches make tight little braids. You can also make Crossed Stockinette, which is a little looser, by knitting in back loops and purling plain, or purling in back loops and knitting plain.

Work some more rows in plain Stockinette Stitch and try a few other things. Somewhere on either a knit or purl row, *slip* a stitch—that is, pass it directly from the left needle to the right needle without drawing any new loop through it. Always slip a stitch, on any row, by inserting the right needle into it *as if to purl,* or purlwise (from behind), *unless* the directions tell you to slip as if to knit, or knitwise, in which case you insert the right needle into it from in front. Notice that when you slip a stitch, the working yarn passes horizontally across this stitch without becoming caught in it. If you hold the working yarn in back, in Knitting Position, while slipping, it crosses the slip-stitch behind. This is called "slip one with yarn in back," or sl 1 wyib (*Figure 17*). If you hold the working yarn in front, in Purling Position, while slipping, it crosses the slip-stitch in front. This is called "slip one with yarn in front," or sl 1 wyif (*Figure 18*). After slipping wyib, the yarn may be either kept in back for knitting the next stitch or brought to the front for purling the next stitch. After slipping wyif, the yarn may be either kept in front for purling the next stitch or taken to the back for knitting the next stitch. One of the greatest advantages of Continental-style knitting is that changing from Knitting Position to Purling Position, or vice versa, is extremely easy; it's just a matter of moving the left forefinger a fraction of an inch forward or back, which takes no time at all. In American-style knitting, on the other hand (literally), changing from Knitting Position to Purling Position requires a whole extra motion of the right hand to pass the yarn between the needle points, which is much more cumbersome.

FIGURE 17—*Sl 1 wyib*

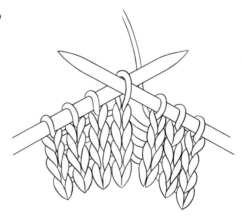

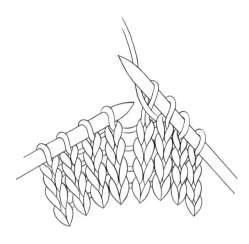

FIGURE 18—*Sl 1 wyif*

Now try a yarn-over (yo). Knit (or purl) a few stitches, then pause and take the yarn once over the top of the right needle, from front to back, before working the next stitch. This puts an extra strand on the needle (*Figure 19*) between two stitches. Below this extra strand, a hole will be left. The extra yo strand is usually worked as a new stitch, and therefore it is an increase (inc), adding one more stitch to the row. If the next stitch after the yo is to be knitted, you just leave the yarn in back, in Knitting Position. If the next stitch after the yo is to be purled,

FIGURE 19—*Yo*

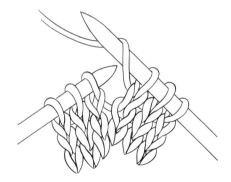

you bring the yarn under the right needle to the front again, to Purling Position. Here again, Continental-style knitting can be a time-saver.

With your Stockinette Stitch swatch in hand, read through the Glossary in this book and try out some other techniques, the descriptions of which you are now prepared to understand. Of course there's a lot more to knitting than just knitting and purling. But once you have thoroughly grasped these two basic techniques, all the others come easily. By the time you've finished your Learn-To-Knit Afghan, you'll know all about those others and can sail through any knitting directions with confidence and expertise.

CASTING ON, METHOD 2

The method of casting on that you have been using is a good all-purpose method. It gives a firm but elastic edge, and it works fast. But it has two disadvantages, both of which can be overcome by learning another, slower method. This is Method 2, otherwise known as the Cable Cast-On. Now that you know how to knit, you are ready to learn it.

The first disadvantage of Method 1 is its long free-end tail. When you come to a project that requires casting on many stitches, you'll find that it's not always easy to plan the length of the free-end tail. You may come to the end of the tail before gaining the necessary number of stitches, which means starting all over again. Or, you may overcompensate with an enormously long tail, which wastes yarn. The second disadvantage of Method 1 is that it cannot be used for casting on stitches in the middle or at the end of a row, as you will want to do when making buttonholes, pockets, other garment details and some types of patterns. Therefore, you will sometimes need Method 2, because it *can* be used at the beginning, or middle, or end of a row, and it *does* start at the free end of the yarn, without any tail to worry about.

Beginning only about 6 inches from the free end of the yarn, cast on 2 stitches with Method 1. Put the needle into the left hand and take up the yarn in Knitting Position. Take the other needle in the right hand. Insert the right needle from front to back *between* the 2 stitches on the left needle (*not* through the first stitch as if to knit) and draw a loose loop through to the front. Place this loop on left needle, keeping it loose (*Figure 20*). This makes the third stitch. * Insert the right needle from front to back *between* this new loop (both strands) and the second stitch on left needle, and draw another loose loop through to the front (*Figure 21*). Place this loop on left needle, keeping it loose. Repeat the process from * until the desired number of stitches have been cast on. Before placing the last loop on the left needle, bring the working yarn between the needle points to the front, to form a dividing strand between the last stitch and the next-to-last one.

FIGURE 20—*Third Stitch*

FIGURE 21—*Fourth Stitch*

This Cable Cast-On is a variant of an old method called Knitting On, which is done by inserting the right needle into the front of the first stitch on left needle and knitting, in the usual way, a new stitch to be placed on the left needle. The trouble with Knitting On is that it makes a rather loose, sloppy edge; try it and see. The Cable Cast-On, however, gives a good firm edge of double strands twisting beneath the needle like a small horizontal cable, because the right needle draws each new loop from behind 2 strands instead of just one.

BINDING OFF

To finish a piece of knitted fabric, you must bind off the stitches to prevent them from unraveling. To begin a binding-off row, knit the first 2 stitches. * With the left needle, reach across in front of the stitch nearest the point of the right needle (the first stitch), and insert the left needle point into the front of the *second* stitch on right needle (*Figure

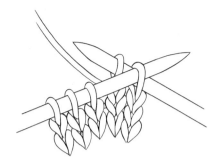

FIGURE 22

22). With the left needle, lift this second stitch up, over the first stitch, and off the right needle altogether (*Figure 23*). Knit one more stitch. Repeat the process from * across the row until all stitches have been bound off and only one loop remains on the right needle. Break the yarn, draw the yarn-end through this last loop, and tighten.

You can also work a binding-off row by *purling,* instead of knitting, the stitches. In either case, the second stitch on the right needle is passed over the first stitch each time in the same way. You can also knit some stitches and purl others in the same row while binding off, according to pattern requirements, or even knit one stitch and purl the next, alternately, while binding off.

FIGURE 23—*One Stitch Bound Off*

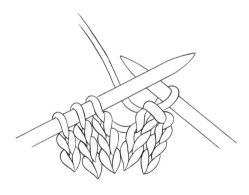

Practice binding off, both knitting and purling, on another swatch *without* breaking the yarn or passing it through the last loop. Just remove the needle from the last loop and pull out the binding-off row, stitch by stitch, taking back or un-knitting onto the left needle as you do so. That way, you can bind off again and again. Pull the bound-off edge from both sides to see if it has as much give as the rest of the knitting. If not, you are binding off too tightly. Practice again, concentrating on binding off more loosely by drawing longer loops up through the passed-over stitches. Another way to bind off loosely is to use a larger-sized needle for the binding-off row than the needle used for the rest of the work.

JOINING NEW STRANDS

To start a new strand of yarn in your work when an old one comes to an end, proceed across the row (any row) until you have about 3 inches of yarn left. Drop this 3-inch tail on the *wrong* side. Take up the new strand, leaving a 3-inch tail of this also on the wrong side, and continue the row. Later, when the row is finished, tie the 2 tails together in a small, firm square knot, drawing the knot up carefully so it is exactly centered on the running-thread between the 2 stitches (the last stitch made with the old strand, and the first stitch made with the new strand).

Always try to place your joining-knots between 2 purl stitches on the wrong side, or 2 knit stitches on the right side—which means the same thing, of course, no matter which side you're working on. Then the knot will be invisible from the right side.

Some knitting teachers forbid knots altogether, because they will show if not carefully placed. But then the student is told to tie the new strand onto the old strand at the beginning or end of a row, which wastes yarn because there might be quite a long piece left over. Also, it's frustrating to start a row, planning to tie on a new strand at the end of it, and find that you don't have enough yarn left to get all the way across. Knots in the middle of a row are really harmless when properly placed.

Of course, when you are starting a row of a different color, the new color is joined by tying it onto the old strand at the beginning of the row, just beneath the needle and as close to the needle as possible.

If you come to a knot in the skein itself, you must cut it out and join the cut ends in the work just as when starting a new skein, because it's very unlikely that such a knot would place itself correctly when drawn into the knitting.

Tails of yarn left over from casting on, binding off or joining, are run through the knitting on the wrong side with the aid of a blunt yarn needle. Run the 2 tails left over from a join in opposite directions from each other, for extra security in keeping the join from coming apart.

HOW TO READ KNITTING DIRECTIONS

Row 1 (right side)—K3, * p1, k4, (p1, k1) twice, p1, k6, (p2, k1) 3 times, p3, k8; rep from *, end p2, k3.

Does that look mysterious to you? Actually the only mysterious thing about it is the question of what sort of pattern it would make; it's a random, never-never line of directions invented on the spur of the moment just to demonstrate some knitting abbreviations. The k's and p's, of course, mean knit and purl. The numbers following each k or p refer to the number of stitches to be knitted or purled. "Row 1 (right side)" tells you that the first pattern row is a right-side row in this case, and therefore all other odd-numbered rows are also right-side rows. "Rep" means "repeat"; and "rep from *" means that after you have knitted the 8 stitches at the end of the line (the final "k8"), you must go back to the first asterisk (*), and begin with "p1, k4 . . ." etc. The first 3 stitches of the row ("k3" before the first asterisk) are edge stitches; they are worked only once, to start, and are not used again as you repeat the directions. Similarly, the last 5 stitches ("end p2, k3" after the second asterisk) are also edge stitches; they are worked *only* at the very end of the row.

All clear so far. But how about those parentheses in the middle of the row? In fact the parentheses are only a way of shortening the directions so that the line of print does not become too long. The material inside each set of parentheses is repeated *consecutively* as many times as directed right after the parentheses. So "(p1, k1) twice" really means "p1, k1, p1, k1." And "(p2, k1) 3 times" really means "p2, k1, p2, k1, p2, k1." This custom of putting parentheses around blocks of repetitive material makes the directions a little easier to read without losing your place. Let's try another example.

Row 1 (wrong side)—P2, k1, * p3, k4, (p2, k2) 4 times, p1, k6; rep from *, end last repeat k4.

In this case the first pattern row is a wrong-side row; therefore all other odd-numbered rows are also wrong-side rows. But notice the wording at the *end* of this row. It doesn't say simply "end so-and-so" like the first example; it says "end *last repeat* so-and-so." This means that there are *no* extra edge stitches at the end of the row; instead, there are 2 stitches *less* than a full pattern, so the final repeat must end with "k4" instead of "k6" as given just before the second asterisk.

Now how do you know exactly how many edge stitches there will be at the beginning and/or end of each row? This brings us to the subject of multiples. Nearly all knitted fabric patterns, except those that can be worked on any number of stitches like basic Garter Stitch or basic Stockinette Stitch, have their own *multiples* of stitches that will make the pattern come out even. These multiples are given at the beginning of each set of pattern directions, like this: "Multiple of 12 sts plus 3," or "Multiple of 18 sts plus 4." The first of these can be worked on any multiple of 12 stitches plus 3 extra edge stitches; that is, on 15, 27, 39, 51, 63 or 75 stitches. The second of these can be worked on any multiple of 18 stitches plus 4 extra edge stitches; that is, on 22, 40, 58 or 76 stitches, and so on. Some patterns have no edge stitches at all, so their directions say simply "Multiple of 10 sts" or "Multiple of 15 sts."

When you are following directions that give you a specific number of stitches to cast on, as in the directions for this afghan, you don't have to pay much attention to the multiples. They are already figured out for you, and the pattern directions will fit into the specified number of cast-on stitches. But whenever you want to use the same pattern on a larger or smaller number of stitches, then you need to know the right multiple with which to begin. Suppose that while working this afghan you find a pattern that you like so much that you want to use it in a sweater. The pattern is worked on a multiple of 10 sts plus 5, and the afghan square has 45 stitches, or 4 pattern repeats. If you measure the width of one pattern repeat and find that you need at least 10 of them to make a piece wide enough for the back of a sweater, you just multiply accordingly, and cast on 105 stitches for your sweater. This is still 10 plus 5, and the directions will work for this larger number just as well as for the smaller number. That's why the added convenience of information on multiples is given with all of these patterns.

There are some kinds of patterns for which multiples are given but are not necessary. Mosaic patterns are an outstanding example of this. Any mosaic pattern can be worked on any number of stitches at all. You simply repeat the directions for each row until you run out of stitches at the end of the row, no matter where in the directions this may happen. (Just remember, in a mosaic pattern, to *knit* the very last stitch of every row, even if the directions call for a slip-stitch in that position.) Since the wrong-side rows of mosaic patterns are exact copies of the preceding right-side rows, it doesn't matter how the pattern is arranged at the left-hand edge.

Then there are other kinds of patterns that have no "multiple" directions, but instead say "Panel of 16 sts" or "Panel of 19 sts." These patterns are relatively narrow, vertical designs, like cables, worked on just a few stitches somewhere in the midst of the knitting. To keep panel designs properly placed, you can insert a pair of markers on the needle, the markers having exactly as many stitches between them as the number of stitches in the panel. The directions for the panel pattern apply *only* to the stitches between the two markers. On each side, beyond the markers, you can work different fabric patterns or different panels. The classic fisherman sweater, showing different kinds of cables side by side, is one example of a contrasting-panel arrangement.

Sometimes, similar rows are contracted in the directions for the sake of brevity and convenience. A pattern may begin like this: Row 1 (wrong side) and all other wrong-side rows—Purl. This means that every wrong-side row throughout the pattern is simply purled straight across, so the wrong-side rows are not referred to again because there is no necessity to repeat this direction every time. Or, a pattern may begin like this: Rows 1, 3, and 5 (right side)—K3, * yo, k1, yo, k3, sl 1—k2 tog—psso, k3; rep from *. This means that the first 3 right-side rows are all alike, so the direction is given just once for all 3 of them. Notice, too, that the directions end right after the second asterisk in this case, which means that although there are 3 extra edge stitches at the beginning of the row, there are no extra edge stitches at the end; the pattern comes out even at the finish of the row.

In general, the reading of pattern directions is a very simple, common-sense sort of process. The main thing is to read *carefully*. Use a ruler or some other straight edge on the page to cover extraneous lines of print and show you only the row you're working on. Also, jot down row numbers, as you work them, on a separate piece of paper. Then when you pause in your knitting, you can pick it up again without losing your place in the pattern.

THE
LEARN-TO-KNIT
AFGHAN

To make this afghan, you'll need the following materials:

80 ounces of knitting worsted weight yarn (20 4-ounce skeins) in 4 colors, as follows:

28 ounces (7 4-ounce skeins) of Color A, a light color

28 ounces (7 4-ounce skeins) of Color B, another light color

12 ounces (3 4-ounce skeins) of Color C, a dark color

12 ounces (3 4-ounce skeins) of Color D, another dark color

12 extra ounces (3 4-ounce skeins) of a 5th contrasting color, if desired, for borders

1 pair straight knitting needles size 6, 10" long

1 circular needle size 6, 16" long

1 set of 4 double-pointed needles size 6

1 blunt yarn needle

1 box of ring markers

1 pair scissors

1 crochet hook size H, if desired, for crocheted borders

Directions for each afghan square tell you which colors to use. Squares are numbered from 1 to 63 throughout all 8 Sections, but you don't necessarily have to work them in this order. You can skip around a little if you like; but be sure to check off the squares that have been worked as you work them, so you won't find yourself doing the same square twice.

The Learn-To-Knit Afghan attempts to do what has probably never been done before, to combine all kinds of knitting techniques in a single project. By the time you finish it, you will know something about the enormous variety of fabrics that knitting can make, and you will be firmly grounded in a basic knowledge of the techniques that make them. Some of the patterns in this afghan are old classics that have been used for centuries; others are original inventions. To give a sampling of both, as well as a survey course in all aspects of knitting, much care has gone into the selection of these patterns.

One other thing that the Learn-To-Knit Afghan teaches you is that stitch and row gauges (numbers of stitches and rows to the inch) are exceedingly variable in different patterns. Even though all squares are approximately the same size when finished, and even though all squares are worked with the same size yarn and needles, the stitch and row counts show wide variations, from a minimum of 30 stitches to a maximum of 58 stitches, and from a minimum of 32 rows to a maximum of 84 rows. Clearly, this tells you that any given pattern requires a different number of stitches and rows from any other, to cover the same area, even though yarn and needle sizes do not change. This conclusively proves that it's essential to test the gauge of every pattern before using it in any of your future knitting projects, by making a preliminary swatch and measuring the number of stitches and rows to the inch. Form this good habit early, and stick to it, so you will never have to suffer the disappointment of having your hand-knitted garments come out too large or too small later on. Suppose, for example, that you want to make the back of a sweater 20″ wide, designed for a pattern that gives 4 stitches to the inch, making a total of 80 stitches, in a different pattern that works more tightly and gives 6 stitches to the inch. If you keep the original number of stitches, 80, your sweater-back will be only a little over 13" wide, and obviously will not fit the person it's intended for! Or again, suppose that the 20" sweater-back is designed for a pattern that gives 7 stitches to the inch, making a total of 140 stitches, and you change to a looser pattern giving 5 stitches to the inch; then the original number of stitches will make your piece 28" wide instead of 20". So you can see that any change likely to affect the gauge of your knitting, whether it be a change in yarn, needle size, knitter or pattern, necessitates the making of a test swatch to determine the right number of stitches for the desired number of inches. *Always* start each future knitting project with a test swatch, measure the number of stitches and rows to the inch on this swatch, and multiply accordingly.

A word about colors: if you prefer to make your afghan in many different colors, instead of following the 4-color system given in the directions, you can certainly do it. If you are a knitter with a big box full of leftover yarn scraps, this is a good opportunity to use them up. Just be sure that all the yarn you use is knitting worsted weight, and that you use 2 strongly contrasting colors, one dark and one light, in every 2-color square.

At the beginning of the directions for each one of these afghan squares, the abbreviations for the techniques used in that particular square are given. Whenever you see an abbreviation that looks unfamiliar, turn back at once to the Glossary and re-read the description of that technique. Before starting the afghan square, cast on a few stitches and practice the technique. This is important. The whole purpose of making a Learn-To-Knit Afghan is to master all of the various operations used in knitting, so you will never be puzzled by any directions that you might encounter in the future. The only way to learn anything in knitting is to *do* it. Read the instructions with yarn and needles in your hands, and practice as you read. If it doesn't look right, try it again.

Even directions that seem unclear when you simply read them will become clear when you follow them with your needles.

Before beginning your afghan, read the Glossary carefully enough to have a good general idea of what's in it. As you work, read it again and again, practicing each new technique as it comes along. In the end you will discover that it's not such a very long jump from beginner to expert knitter, after all.

GLOSSARY OF TECHNIQUES

SECTION I—*KNIT-PURL COMBINATIONS*

k   knit. Any number following "k" is the number of stitches to be knitted consecutively, as k1, k2, k3, etc.

p   purl. Any number following "p" is the number of stitches to be purled consecutively, as p1, p2, p3, etc.

k-b   knit in *back* loop of stitch(es), inserting needle from the right to emerge on the left side of the back loop, and knit a new stitch from that position. K1-b, k2-b, k3-b, etc.

p-b   purl in *back* loop of stitch(es), inserting needle from behind the stitch to the left of the back loop, to emerge to the right of the front loop, and wrap yarn over the needle in front to complete the purl stitch in the usual way. P1-b, p2-b, p3-b, etc.

k in row below   knit, not into the first stitch on left needle, but into the front of the loop directly below that stitch, thus taking 2 loops at once off the left needle instead of just one. "Purl in row below" is the same thing backward, with the needle inserted into the lower loop from behind and the yarn wrapped over the needle in front to purl in the usual way.

st   stitch.

SECTION II—*MOSAIC PATTERNS*

sl   slip. Pass stitch(es) from left needle to right needle without working. The right needle is always inserted into the stitch(es) from behind, as if to purl or purlwise, unless directions specify as if to knit or knitwise, which means that the right needle is inserted from in front. Sl 1, sl 2, sl 3, etc.

sl-st   slip-stitch; a stitch that has been slipped.

wyib   with yarn in back. While slipping stitch(es), the working yarn is held behind the left needle in Knitting Position, so the strand crosses the slip-stitch on the side away from the knitter. Sl 1 wyib, sl 2 wyib, etc.

wyif   with yarn in front. While slipping stitch(es), the working yarn is held in front of the left needle in Purling Position, so the strand crosses the slip-stitch on the side toward the knitter. Sl 1 wyif, sl 2 wyif, etc.

SECTION III—*SLIP-STITCH PATTERNS*

k wrapping twice   insert needle into stitch as if to knit, wrap yarn twice around needle point instead of just once, and withdraw needle bringing both loops through stitch. The extra wrap is usually dropped on the next row, to elongate the stitch. "Purl wrapping twice" is the same thing backward; the needle comes through the stitch to the front, and the yarn is wrapped twice over the needle point.

drop   let a stitch, or a strand, or an extra loop of a double-wrapped stitch, fall from the left needle. (Beginners often think "dropping a stitch" is a terrible mistake, but it is a legitimate technique used in a number of patterns.)

SECTION IV—*TWIST-STITCH PATTERNS*

RT   Right Twist; 2 stitches twisted so that the one on the right side of the fabric moves diagonally from left to right. There are 2 ways to work it:

> *Method 1*—skip 1 st and knit the 2nd st on the left needle in front loop, then knit the skipped st in front loop; slip both sts from needle together.
> *Method 2*—knit 2 sts together in front loops, leave on left needle; insert right needle between the 2 sts just knitted together, and knit the first st again; slip both sts from needle together.

LT   Left Twist; 2 stitches twisted so that the one on the right side of the fabric moves diagonally from right to left. There are 2 ways to work it:

> *Method 1*—skip 1 st and knit the 2nd st on left needle in back loop, then knit the skipped st in front loop; slip both sts from needle together.
> *Method 2*—skip 1 st and knit the 2nd st on left needle in back loop, then knit the skipped st and the 2nd st together in back loops; slip both sts from needle together.

PRT   Purl Right Twist; a Right Twist worked from the wrong side of the fabric. Skip 1 st and purl the 2nd st on left needle, then purl the skipped st and the 2nd st together; slip both sts from needle together.

PLT   Purl Left Twist; a Left Twist worked from the wrong side of the fabric. Skip 1 st and purl the 2nd st on left needle in back loop (inserting right needle through this back loop from the left, behind, and reaching around skipped st to wrap yarn in front and purl); then purl the skipped st; slip both sts from needle together.

Tw 3 Twist Three; Knit into front of 3rd st on left needle, then into 2nd st, then into first st; slip all 3 sts from needle together. "Tw 4" is done the same way, starting with the 4th st on left needle.

SECTION V—*CABLES*

dpn double-pointed needle or cable needle. In cabling, sts are slipped onto one end of the dpn and worked off the other end.

FC Front Cross; a cable crossing in which the dpn with its sts is left in front of the work while other sts are knitted, so that the sts on the right side of the fabric move diagonally from right to left. Numbers of sts involved in the crossing are given with pattern notes.

BC Back Cross; a cable crossing in which the dpn with its sts is left in back of the work while other sts are knitted, so that the sts on the right side of the fabric move diagonally from left to right. Numbers of sts involved in the crossing are given with pattern notes.

FPC Front Purl Cross; a Front Cross in which the background sts (worked before the sts on dpn) are purled. Numbers of sts involved in the crossing are given with pattern notes.

BPC Back Purl Cross; a Back Cross in which the background sts (worked after the sts on dpn) are purled. Numbers of sts involved in the crossing are given with pattern notes.

1. *Single Increases:* making 2 stitches from 1 stitch, or creating 1 new stitch

inc   knit once into the front loop, then once into the back loop, of the same stitch.

purl inc   purl once into the front loop, then once into the back loop, of the same stitch.

k under running thread   insert right needle from front under the running thread between the st just worked and the next st, and knit. "Purl under running thread" is the same thing backward, with the needle inserted from behind under the running thread and the yarn wrapped over the needle in front to purl a new stitch.

M1   Make One. Insert right needle from behind under running thread and lift it up onto point of left needle; then knit one st into the back loop of this thread.

yo   yarn over. Take the working yarn once over the top of the right needle, from front to back, before working the next st. If the next st after the yo is to be knitted, the yarn remains behind, in Knitting Position. If the next st after the yo is to be purled, the yarn comes under the needle to the front, to Purling Position. A yo makes a hole and is usually worked as a new, separate stitch on the return row.

2. *Double Increases:* making 3 stitches from 1 stitch, or creating 2 new stitches

double inc   knit once into the *back* loop, then once into the *front* loop, of the same st, and slip these 2 new sts from left needle; then insert left needle point behind the vertical strand that runs downward from between the 2 sts just made and knit into the *back* of this strand to make the 3rd st of the group.

(k1, p1, k1) knit, purl, and knit into the same stitch. Knit, leaving st on left needle; bring yarn to front and purl into the same st, still leaving it on left needle; take yarn to back and again knit into the same st; slip all 3 sts from needle together.

(k1, yo, k1) knit, yarn-over, and knit again into the same stitch. Knit, leaving st on left needle; take yarn once over the top of right needle; knit again into the same st; slip all 3 sts from needle together.

yo2 double yarn over. Take yarn once over the top of the right needle, under to the front, and over again to the back before working next knit st, or once more under to the front if the next st is to be purled. Double yarn-overs may be worked as 2 new, separate stitches on the return row, by working (k1, p1) or (p1, k1) into the long loop; or, one of the loops may be dropped on the return row, to elongate the stitch.

3. *Multiple Increases:* making more than 3 stitches from 1 stitch, or creating more than 2 new stitches

(k1, yo, k1, yo, k1) 5 sts made from one, as follows: * knit into the st, yarn over right needle; repeat from * once more; then knit into the st again and slip all 5 sts from needle together.

(k1, yo, k1, yo, k1, yo, k1) 7 sts made from one, as follows: * knit into the st, yarn over right needle; repeat from * twice more; then knit into the st again and slip all 7 sts from needle together.

yo3 triple yarn over. Like a yo2, with one more wrap.

yo4 quadruple yarn over. Like a yo2, with 2 more wraps.

4. *Single Decreases:* making 1 stitch from 2 stitches

k2 tog knit 2 sts together as one st, inserting right needle from front through the 2nd and first sts on left needle, in that order, and knitting 1 st. "K2 tog" makes a decrease slanting to the *right* on the knit side of the work.

p2 tog   purl 2 sts together as one st, inserting right needle from be-hind through the first and 2nd sts on left needle, in that order, and purling 1 st. "P2 tog" makes a decrease slanting to the *right* on the knit side of the work.

k2 tog-b   knit 2 sts together as one st through back loops, inserting right needle from the right through the first and 2nd sts on left needle, in that order, and knitting 1 st. "K2 tog-b" makes a decrease slanting to the *left* on the knit side of the work.

ssk   slip, slip, knit. Slip 2 sts *knitwise,* one at a time; then insert point of left needle into the fronts of these 2 slipped sts, and knit them together from this position. "Ssk" makes a decrease slanting to the *left* on the knit side of the work, and forms a symmetrical match for "k2 tog."

sl 1–k1–psso   slip 1, knit 1, pass slipped st over. Slip 1 st *knitwise,* knit next st, then with left needle draw the slipped st over the knit st and off right needle. "Sl 1–k1–psso" makes a decrease slanting to the *left* on the knit side of the work, and is an older and less efficient form of "ssk."

p2 tog-b   purl 2 sts together as one st through back loops, inserting right needle from behind through the 2nd and first sts on left needle, in that order, so that the needle point emerges in front to the right of the front strand of the first st; then wrap yarn over the needle in front to complete the purl st in the usual way. "P2 tog-b" makes a decrease slanting to the *left* on the knit side of the work, and forms a match for "p2 tog."

5. *Double Decreases:* making 1 stitch from 3 stitches

k3 tog   knit 3 sts together as one st, inserting right needle from front through the 3rd, 2nd, and first sts on left needle, in that order, and knitting 1 st. "K3 tog" makes a decrease slanting to the *right* on the knit side of the work.

p3 tog purl 3 sts together as one st, inserting right needle from behind through the first, 2nd, and 3rd sts on left needle, in that order, and purling 1 st. "P3 tog" makes a decrease slanting to the *right* on the knit side of the work.

k3 tog-b knit 3 sts together as one st through back loops, inserting right needle from the right through the first, 2nd, and 3rd sts on left needle, in that order, and knitting 1 st. "K3 tog-b" makes a decrease slanting to the *left* on the knit side of the work.

p3 tog-b purl 3 sts together as one st through back loops, inserting right needle from behind through the 3rd, 2nd, and first sts on left needle, in that order, and wrapping yarn over the needle point in front to complete the purl st in the usual way. "P3 tog-b" makes a decrease slanting to the *left* on the knit side of the work.

p3 tog-b (alternative method)   p2 tog, return the resulting st to left needle; then with point of right needle pass the next st over the p2-tog st and off left needle; slip the st back to right needle. This is the same as "sl 1–k2 tog–psso" worked from the wrong side.

sl 1–k2 tog–psso slip 1, knit 2 together, pass slipped st over. Slip 1 st *knitwise,* knit next 2 sts together, then with left needle draw the slipped st over the k2-tog st and off right needle. This makes a central decrease with the right-hand stitch prominent.

sl 2–k1-p2sso slip 2, knit 1, pass 2 slipped sts over. Slip 2 sts at once, knitwise, inserting needle as if to k2 tog; knit next st, then with left needle draw the 2 slipped sts *together* over the knit st and off right needle. This makes a central decrease with the middle stitch prominent.

6. Multiple decreases: making 1 stitch from 4 or more stitches

p5 tog purl 5 sts together as one st, inserting needle from behind through all 5 sts at once and wrapping yarn over the needle in front to complete the purl st in the usual way. Other multiple decreases: 4 or more sts may be knitted together through front or back loops; or some sts may be slipped, others worked together, and the slipped sts passed over, as in "sl 1–k2 tog–psso."

MB   Make Bobble. A bobble is a knot-like formation made by increasing in one st, working back and forth on the increased sts, then decreasing to one st again; directions are given with pattern notes.

turn   to work short rows on a bobble or in shaping, turn the work around just as when reaching the end of a row, wherever the direction "turn" is given in the middle of a row.

SECTION VIII—*SPECIAL TECHNIQUES*

pass   to reach with left needle to a st already one or more sts away from point of right needle, lift it over the intervening st or sts and off right needle, as in "psso" or when binding off.

dip   a stitch made by inserting right needle through a st several rows below the row on the needles, and drawing a loop through as if knitting.

pick up   with the right side of the work facing, holding yarn behind in Knitting Position, poke the right needle from front through the fabric 2 strands in from the edge, and draw a loop of working yarn through to the front and onto right needle. Picking up stitches is like knitting without a left-hand needle, as picked-up loops are placed on right needle one at a time.

round   directions for seamless circular knitting (on a circular needle or a set of double-pointed needles) are given in rounds instead of rows. One round goes once around the circle and back to the starting point, usually indicated by a marker.

SECTION I—KNIT-PURL COMBINATIONS

Now that you've learned how to cast on, knit, purl and bind off, you are ready to enter the wonderful world of knitting patterns. You'll be surprised to see how easily you can make beautiful fabric designs with just these simple, basic techniques. Knit-purl combinations are used by every knitter, but they are especially enjoyable for the beginner since they offer easy but valuable practice in reading directions, counting stitches and becoming familiar with the inimitable look and feel of hand-knitting.

Incredible as it may seem, there are people who have knitted for years and still cannot tell the difference between a knit stitch and a purl stitch on the needle. You must train yourself to see this difference instantly. Watching the stitches as you work knit-purl patterns is a good way to do this. The secret is to look at the arrangement of strands *just below* the loop that passes over the needle. A stitch that has been knitted on the present row (or purled on the preceding row) emerges from a little V of two strands below the needle. A stitch that has been purled on the present row (or knitted on the preceding row) emerges from behind a single strand that lies horizontally across the base of the stitch and forms a little bump there.

If you aspire to become a truly expert knitter, remember that you must knit with your eyes as well as with your hands. Always watch what you are doing! And remember—every knit stitch worked on one side of the fabric makes a purl stitch on the other side, while every purl stitch worked on one side of the fabric makes a knit stitch on the other side. When you knit a row, you are, at the same time, making a purled row on the back of the work (the side you're *not looking* at). When you purl a row, you are, at the same time, making a knit row on the back of the work.

Square 1: **Striped Garter Stitch**

Colors A and C. Technique: k
Multiple: any number of stitches

With A, cast on 39 stitches. Knit one row. This is the first *wrong-side* row. It makes the first stripe of Color A. Now join C; that is, tie the Color C strand onto the Color A strand just below the needle.

SQUARE 1: *Striped Garter Stitch*

* With C, knit 2 rows. Drop C strand in front, toward you, pick up A strand behind. With A, knit 2 rows. Drop A strand in front, pick up C strand behind. Repeat these 4 rows from * until there are 39 2-row stripes, 19 stripes of Color C and 20 stripes of Color A, counting the first wrong-side row. Break C. Bind off on the right side with A, knitting all stitches as you bind off.

Study your Garter Stitch square. It is the basis for many different kinds of patterns that you will encounter later. Notice that on the right side of the work, where the colors changed every other row, the stripes are sharp and clear, while on the wrong side they blend together. This shows that whenever you are working with two colors, you should knit the first row of each new strand on the right side for a sharp stripe. Also, you should always change colors at the right-hand edge as described above: drop the strand that you have just used in front, toward you, and pick up the other strand behind.

When Garter Stitch is worked in one color only, you can't tell the right side from the wrong side because both sides look alike.

Notice too that the Garter Stitch square is square because it has exactly as many 2-row stripes as the number of stitches cast on. This means that each stitch is as wide as two rows are high. So any piece of Garter Stitch worked to the same number of 2-row ridges (that is, twice as many rows) as there are stitches, will be a square.

Garter Stitch lies flat, doesn't curl, doesn't require pressing or blocking, and therefore is very useful for borders, collars, cuffs, button bands and other portions of garments where a non-curling fabric is needed.

(Opposite) SQUARE 2: *Striped Stockinette Stitch*

Square 2: **Striped Stockinette Stitch**

Colors B and D. Techniques: k, p
Multiple: any number of stitches

With B, cast on 41 stitches. Purl one row. This is the first *wrong-side* row. It makes the first stripe of Color B. Now join D, tying the Color D strand onto the Color B strand as in Square 1.

    * With D, knit one row, purl one row. Drop D strand in front, pick up

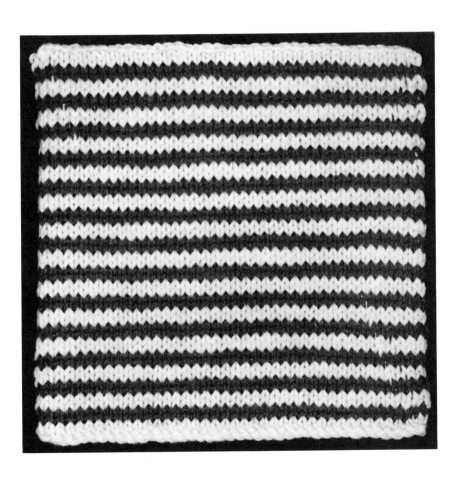

B strand behind. With B, knit one row, purl one row. Drop B strand in front, pick up D strand behind. Repeat these 4 rows from * until there are 27 2-row stripes, 13 stripes of Color D and 14 stripes of Color B counting the first wrong-side row. Break D. Bind off on the right side with B, knitting all stitches as you bind off.

Study your Stockinette Stitch square. This is the basic sock-and-sweater fabric. The stripes are clear on the right side, blended together on the wrong side, just as in striped Garter Stitch. But Stockinette Stitch looks different on the right and wrong sides, even if it is worked in a single color. The right, or knit, side is smooth; the wrong, or purl, side is bumpy, showing little half-moon-shaped loops for every stitch.

Notice too that the Stockinette Stitch square has a couple of stitches more, and several rows less, than the Garter Stitch square, even though its final proportions are the same. Stockinette Stitch covers more ground lengthwise, row for row, than Garter Stitch, because its stitches are laid out flat instead of crinkled up into horizontal ridges. Therefore you need fewer rows of Stockinette Stitch to reach any given length.

Doubtless you have already noticed that Stockinette Stitch *curls*—toward you at the top and bottom, away from you at the sides. Even blocking and pressing will not fully control this tendency. That's why garments made of Stockinette Stitch always need borders of some non-curling fabric at their exposed edges.

Square 3: **Basketweave**

Color B. Techniques: k, p
Multiple of 8 stitches plus 3

Cast on 43 stitches.
Row 1 (wrong side)—Purl.

SQUARE 3: *Basketweave*

Row 2—K3, * p5, k3; rep from *.
Row 3—P3, * k5, p3; rep from *.
Row 4—Repeat Row 2.
Row 5—Purl.
Row 6—P4, * k3, p5; rep from *, end last repeat p4.
Row 7—K4, * p3, k5; rep from *, end last repeat k4.
Row 8—Repeat Row 6.

Repeat Rows 1–8 seven times, then Rows 1–4 again (60 rows). Bind off on wrong side, purling all stitches.

Basketweave is a classic fabric for all kinds of knitted articles. It doesn't curl, looks very attractive, and is easy to work.

Square 4: **Lattice with Seed Stitch**

Color B. Techniques: k, p
Multiple of 14 stitches plus 12

Cast on 40 stitches.
    Row 1 (wrong side)—Purl.
    Rows 2, 4, 6, and 8—(P1, k1) twice, p1, * k2, (p1, k1) twice, p1; rep from *.
    Rows 3, 5, and 7—(P1, k1)twice, * p4, k1, p1, k1; rep from *, end p1.
    Row 9—K5, * p2, k12; rep from *, end last repeat k5.
    Row 10—P5, * k2, p12; rep from *, end last repeat p5.
    Rows 11 through 18—Repeat Rows 1 through 8.
    Row 19—K12, * p2, k12; rep from *.
    Row 20—P12, * k2, p12; rep from *.

Repeat Rows 1–20 twice, then Rows 1–18 again (58 rows). Bind off on wrong side, purling all stitches.

Between the vertical knit ribs and the horizontal purled welts in this pattern there are blocks of Seed Stitch, a popular basic knit-purl fabric created by a "k1, p1" that reverses on every row. Like Garter Stitch, Seed Stitch will not curl and is useful for borders.

SQUARE 4: *Lattice with Seed Stitch*

Square 5: **Diagonal Ribbing**

Color A. Techniques: k, p
Multiple of 4 stitches plus 1

Cast on 49 stitches.

Rows 1 and 3—P1, * k2, p2; rep from *.

Rows 2 and 4— * K2, p2; rep from *, end k1.

Rows 5 and 7—* P2, k2; rep from *, end p1.

Rows 6 and 8—K1, * p2, k2; rep from *.

Rows 9 and 11—Repeat Rows 6 and 8.

Rows 10 and 12—Repeat Rows 5 and 7.

Rows 13 and 15—Repeat Rows 2 and 4.

Rows 14 and 16—Repeat Rows 1 and 3.

SQUARE 5: *Diagonal Ribbing*

Repeat Rows 1–16 three times, then Rows 1–3 again (51 rows). Bind off on Row 4, knitting over the knit stitches and purling over the purl stitches.

There is no specified right side or wrong side for this pattern, because it looks the same on both sides, except for one circumstance that appears, at first glance, very curious indeed. On the side that has the odd-numbered rows, the diagonal ribs slant upward to the left. Flip the knitted square over and you will see that on the even-numbered side the diagonal ribs slant upward to the right! Think about this for a little while, until you have grasped its simple explanation for yourself.

Diagonal Ribbing makes a pretty variation on the conventional k2, p2 ribbing usually seen in sweater borders. It may be used also for an entire garment. Watch the formation of knit stitches and purl stitches carefully as you work this pattern, and you will soon see how to move the ribs one stitch over every fourth row, without having to refer back to the directions.

Square 6: **Twisted and Crossed Ribbing**

Color B. Techniques: k, p, k-b, p-b
Multiple of 4 stitches plus 2

Cast on 46 stitches.
　　Rows 1, 3, 5, 7, and 9 (right side)—K2-b, * p2, k2-b; rep from *.
　　Rows 2, 4, 6, 8, and 10—P2-b, * k2, p2-b; rep from *.
　　Rows 11, 13, 15, 17, and 19—P2, * k2-b, p2; rep from *.
　　Rows 12, 14, 16, 18, and 20—K2, * p2, k2; rep from *.

Repeat Rows 1–20 twice, then Rows 1–13 again (53 rows). Bind off on wrong side, knitting over knit stitches and purling over purl stitches.

Plain k2, p2 ribbing, which looks the same on both sides, is the most commonly used border pattern for sweaters. This square gives two attractive variations, which you may substitute for k2, p2 ribbing for a more interesting touch in any garment. Rows 1–10 make twisted ribs, in which the stitches are worked through the back loops on both right-side and wrong-side rows; Rows 11–20 make crossed ribs, in which the stitches are worked through the back loops on right-side rows only.

SQUARE 6: *Twisted and Crossed Ribbing*

In this square you can see that twisted ribs look like tight little braids; crossed ribs are looser, though not so loose as plain ribbing. Working a stitch through its back loop causes it to cross at the base. The strand on the right-hand side of the stitch passes over to the left-hand side of the next stitch above, and vice versa. Whenever it is desirable to keep stitches from looking too loose and open, working in the back loops will help to close them up.

Square 7: **Garter and Rib Pattern**

Color B. Techniques: k, p, k-b, p-b
Multiple of 16 stitches plus 1

Cast on 49 stitches.
  Rows 1, 3, 5, and 7 (right side)—* (K1-b, p1) 4 times, k1-b, p7; rep
    from *, end k1.
  Rows 2, 4, 6, and 8—P1, * p7, (p1-b, k1) 4 times, p1-b; rep from *.
  Rows 9, 11, 13, and 15—K1, * p7, (k1-b, p1) 4 times, k1-b; rep from *.
  Rows 10, 12, 14, and 16—* (P1-b, k1) 4 times, p1-b, p7; rep from *,
    end p1.

Repeat Rows 1–16 three times, then Rows 1–8 again (56 rows). Bind off on right side, purling all stitches.

This pattern is an excellent illustration of the difference in fabric width between Ribbing, which squeezes, and Garter Stitch, which spreads. Each block of Garter Stitch (shown by 4 horizontal ridges) looks wider than each group of 5 ribs above, below, and to each side of it; yet there are only 7 stitches in the Garter Stitch block, and 9 stitches in the group of ribs! Notice, also, how very far out of the ver-

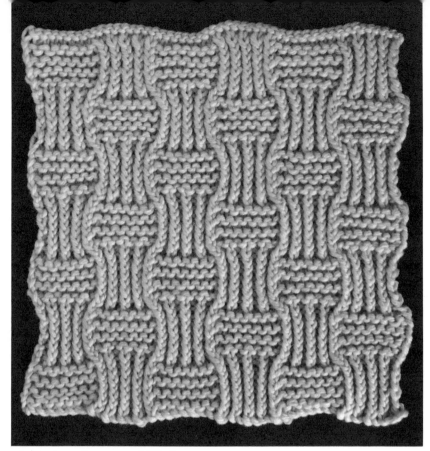

SQUARE 7: *Garter and Rib Pattern*

tical line the continuous ribs are forced to curve, as they are alternately pulled by the Ribbing and pushed by the Garter Stitch.

The important lesson taught by this square is that different patterns can create very obvious differences in *gauge* (number of stitches and rows to the inch), even when worked with the same yarn and needle size.

Square 8: **Rose Fabric**

Colors B and C. Techniques: k, p, k in row below
Multiple: even number of stitches

With B, cast on 30 stitches. Knit one row. Join C.
Row 1 (right side)—With C, k1, * p1, k1 in the row below; rep from
*, end k1.

SQUARE 8: *Rose Fabric*

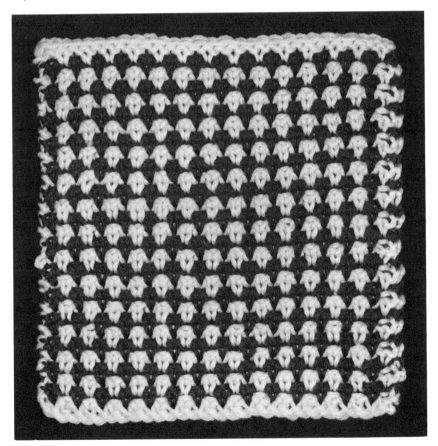

Row 2—With C, knit.
Row 3—With B, k1, * k1 in the row below, p1; rep from *, end k1.
Row 4—With B, knit.

Repeat Rows 1–4 fourteen times (56 rows). Bind off *loosely* on right side with B, knitting all stitches.

Rose Fabric is loose, fluffy, non-curling and has a lot of lateral spread, as you can tell from the relatively small number of stitches required for this square. In this two-color version, the wrong side is also very pretty.

Knitting a stitch in the row below is especially easy to understand when the previous row has been knitted, as here; you just insert the needle from the front under the horizontal "purl strand," from behind which the stitch on the left-hand needle emerges, and knit. Knitting (or purling) in the row below always means that you draw the next stitch from one loop *lower* than the loop that is on the needle, so there are two strands caught in the completed stitch instead of just one.

SECTION II—MOSAIC PATTERNS

Mosaic knitting is a new, easy method of working in two colors, by using only one color at a time and forming the designs with slip-stitches. It differs from other slip-stitch color knitting in various ways:

(1) The two colors are constantly changed, every other row, at the right-hand edge of the knitted piece.

(2) Every wrong-side row is an exact copy of the preceding right-side row. The same color is used to work the same stitches again, while the same slip-stitches, of the other color, are slipped again. The only difference between right-side rows and wrong-side rows is that, on the for-

mer, all slip-stitches are slipped *with yarn in back;* while on the latter, all the same slip-stitches are slipped *with yarn in front.*

(3) Because the wrong-side rows copy the preceding right-side rows, directions can be given for right-side rows only; wrong-side rows do not require them.

(4) Also because the wrong-side rows copy the preceding right-side rows, each mosaic pattern is an "open-ended" pattern, which means that it can be worked on any number of stitches at all. The right-side row does *not* have to end at any particular point in the directions. As you work the pattern, you will find that your row can, and does, end anywhere. Just remember always to *knit* the very last stitch of the row, even if the directions call for a slip-stitch in that position.

Therefore, although multiples are given for your future reference with the patterns in this section, they are hardly needed. You simply repeat each right-side row from the asterisk (*) over and over until you run out of stitches, knitting the last stitch each time.

(5) The stitches that are worked on wrong-side rows may be either knitted or purled. In the first case, the result is a nubby Garter Stitch fabric; in the second, the result is a smooth Stockinette Stitch fabric. Any mosaic pattern can be worked either way. The small sampling of mosaics included in this section will enable you to try both procedures. When mosaic patterns are knitted on the wrong-side rows, their proportion of width to length is just like that of striped Garter Stitch; that is, twice as many rows as the number of stitches will make a square.

Mosaic knitting is a lot of fun for beginners, who usually are delighted to discover that they can make exciting two-color designs with so little trouble and effort. Best of all, because mosaics can be worked on any number of stitches, you can use any pattern that you like to make a garment or other article of any size, just by casting on the number of stitches required for the desired width. You don't have to worry about multiples. Mosaic knitting also offers a limitless choice of unusual and original designs. If, after working the patterns in this section, you'd like to learn more mosaics, you'll find many others in *A Second Treasury of Knitting Patterns, Charted Knitting Designs* and *Sampler Knitting.*

SQUARE 9: *Horizontal Chain*

Square 9: **Horizontal Chain**

Colors B and D. Techniques: k, p, sl wyib, sl wyif
Multiple of 10 stitches

With B, cast on 45 stitches. Purl one row. Join D. Note: on all right-side rows, sl all sl-sts wyib. Always knit the last stitch of the row, which may come at any point in the line of directions.

Row 1 (right side)—With D, * k5, sl 1, k3, sl 1; rep from *.

Row 2 and all other wrong-side rows—With the same color as pre-vious row, purl all the same sts of that color knitted on previous row; sl all the same sl-sts wyif.

Row 3—With B, k4, * sl 1, k5, sl 1, k3; rep from *.

Row 5—With D, k1, * sl 3, k7; rep from *.

Rows 7 and 9—Repeat Rows 3 and 1.

Row 11—With B, k6, * sl 3, k7; rep from *.

Row 12 (wrong side)—See Row 2.

Repeat Rows 1–12 five times, then Rows 1 and 2 again (62 rows). With B, knit one row; then bind off on wrong side, purling all stitches.

This is a simple but very effective pattern of interlocking dark and light motifs, shaped in bold blocks connected by horizontal bands.

Square 10: **Diagonal Chain**

Colors B and D. Techniques: k, p, sl wyib, sl wyif
Multiple of 8 stitches

With B, cast on 46 stitches. Purl one row. Join D. Note: on all right-side rows, sl all sl-sts wyib. Always knit the last stitch of the row, which may come at any point in the line of directions.

SQUARE 10: *Diagonal Chain*

Row 1 (right side)—With D, k2, * sl 1, k5, sl 1, k1; rep from *.

Row 2 and all other wrong-side rows—With the same color as previous row, purl all the same sts of that color knitted on previous row; sl all the same sl-sts wyif.

Row 3—With B, * k5, sl 1, k1, sl 1; rep from *.

Row 5—With D, k2, * sl 1, k1, sl 1, k5; rep from *.

Row 7—With B, * k1, sl 1, k5, sl 1; rep from *.
Row 9—With D, k4, * sl 1, k1, sl 1, k5; rep from *.
Row 11—With B, k1, * sl 1, k1, sl 1, k5; rep from *.
Row 13—With D, k6, * sl 1, k1, sl 1, k5; rep from *.
Row 15—With B, k3, * sl 1, k1, sl 1, k5; rep from *.
Row 16 (wrong side)—See Row 2.

Repeat Rows 1–16 four times, then Rows 1 and 2 again (66 rows).
With B, knit one row; then bind off on wrong side, purling all stitches.

This is an easy mosaic pattern of diagonal stripes, each stripe bearing dots of its opposite color.

Square 11: **Miniature Mosaic**

Colors A and D. Techniques: k, sl wyib, sl wyif
Multiple of 8 stitches

With A, cast on 43 stitches. Knit one row. Join D. Note: on all right-side rows, sl all sl-sts wyib. Always knit the last stitch of the row, which may come at any point in the line of directions.

Row 1 (right side)—With D, k4, * sl 1, k1, sl 1, k5; rep from *.
Row 2 and all other wrong-side rows—With the same color as previous row, knit all the same sts of that color again, and sl all the same sl-sts wyif.
Row 3—With A, k3, * sl 1, k3; rep from *.
Row 5—With D, k2, * sl 1, k5, sl 1, k1; rep from *.
Row 7—With A, k5, * sl 1, k7; rep from *.
Rows 9, 11, and 13—Repeat Rows 5, 3, and 1.
Row 15—With A, k1, * sl 1, k7; rep from *.
Row 16—See Row 2.

Repeat Rows 1–16 five times, then Rows 1 and 2 again (82 rows). With A, knit 2 rows; then bind off on right side, knitting all stitches.

This pattern demonstrates the nubby Garter Stitch type of fabric that results when the wrong-side rows of a Mosaic Pattern are knitted instead of purled. On such wrong-side rows, the yarn is naturally held in back of the work, in knitting position; therefore it must be brought forward between the needle points before slipping each slip-stitch *wyif*, and returned to the back again, to knitting position, after each slip-stitch has been slipped.

SQUARE 11: *Miniature Mosaic*

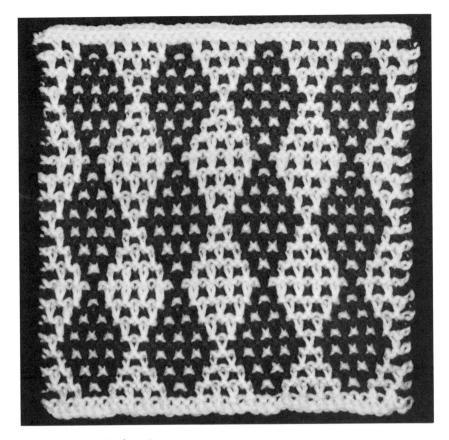

SQUARE 12: *Harlequin*

Square 12: **Harlequin**

Colors A and D. Techniques: k, sl wyib, sl wyif
Multiple of 10 stitches

With A, cast on 43 stitches. Knit one row. Join D. Note: on all right-side rows, sl all sl-sts wyib. Always knit the last stitch of the row, which may come at any point in the line of directions.

Row 1 (right side)—With D, k2, * sl 1, k1, sl 1, k3, (sl 1, k1) twice; rep from *.

Row 2 and all other wrong-side rows—With the same color as previous row, knit all the same sts of that color again, and sl all the same sl-sts wyif.

Row 3—With A, k5, * sl 1, k1, sl 1, k7; rep from *.

Row 5—With D, k1, * sl 1, k1, sl 1, k5, sl 1, k1; rep from *.

Row 7—With A, k4, * (sl 1, k1) twice, sl 1, k5; rep from *.

Row 9—With D, k2, * sl 1, k7, sl 1, k1; rep from *.

Row 11—With A, k3, * (sl 1, k1) 3 times, sl 1, k3; rep from *.

Row 13—With D, k1, * sl 1, k9; rep from *.

Rows 15, 17, 19, 21, 23, and 25—Repeat Rows 11, 9, 7, 5, 3, and 1.

Row 27—With A, k6, * sl 1, k9; rep from *.

Row 28 (wrong side)—see Row 2.

Repeat Rows 1–28 twice, then Rows 1–26 again (82 rows). With A, knit 2 rows; then bind off on right side, knitting all stitches.

Harlequin is a pattern of contrasting diamonds, very good for socks, vests and pillows.

Square 13: **Greek Cross**

Colors A and D. Techniques: k, sl wyib, sl wyif
Multiple of 14 stitches

With A, cast on 43 stitches. Knit one row. Join D. Note: on all right-side rows, sl all sl-sts wyib. Always knit the last stitch of the row, which may come at any point in the line of directions.

Row 1 (right side)—With D, k1, sl 1, * k1, sl 1, (k3, sl 1) twice, k1, sl 3; rep from *.

SQUARE 13: *Greek Cross*

Row 2 and all other wrong-side rows—With the same color as previous row, knit all the same sts of that color again, and sl all the same
sl-sts wyif.

Row 3—With A, k4, * sl 1, k5, sl 1, k7; rep from *.

Row 5—With D, k1, * (sl 1, k3) 3 times, sl 1, k1; rep from *.

Row 7—With A, k2, * sl 1, k3, sl 1, k1, (sl 1, k3) twice; rep from *.

Row 9—With D, k3, * sl 1, k7, sl 1, k5; rep from *.
Row 11—With A, k4, * sl 1, k1, sl 3, k1, (sl 1, k3) twice; rep from *.
Rows 13, 15, 17, and 19—Repeat Rows 9, 7, 5, and 3.
Row 20 (wrong side)—see Row 2.

Repeat Rows 1–20 four times, then Rows 1 and 2 again (82 rows). With A, knit 2 rows; then bind off on right side, knitting all stitches.

Notice how cleverly this pattern alternates dark-on-light and light-on-dark motifs.

Square 14: Chevron

Colors B and C. Techniques: k, sl wyib, sl wyif
Multiple of 14 stitches

With B, cast on 43 stitches. Knit one row. Join C. Note: on all right-side rows, sl all sl-sts wyib. Always knit the last stitch of the row, which may come at any point in the line of directions.

Row 1 (right side)—With C, k1, * (sl 1, k1) twice, sl 1, k3, (sl 1, k1) 3 times; rep from *.

Row 2 and all other wrong-side rows—With the same color as previous row, knit all the same sts of that color again, and sl all the same sl-sts wyif.

Row 3—With B, k6, * sl 1, k1, sl 1, k11; rep from *.
Row 5—With C, k1, * sl 1, k1, sl 1, k7, (sl 1, k1) twice; rep from *.
Row 7—With B, k4, * (sl 1, k1) 3 times, sl 1, k7; rep from *.
Row 9—With C, k1, * sl 1, k11, sl 1, k1; rep from *.
Row 11—With B, k2, * (sl 1, k1) 5 times, sl 1, k3; rep from *.
Row 13—With C, knit.
Rows 15 through 28—Repeat Rows 1 through 14, *reversing colors.*

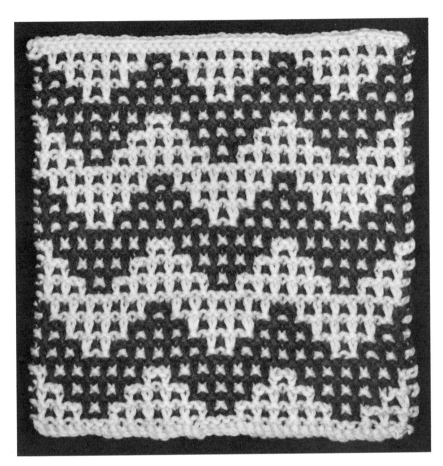

SQUARE 14: *Chevron*

Repeat Rows 1–28 three times (84 rows). Bind off on right side with B, knitting all stitches.

This Chevron pattern may be worked in bands of many different, contrasting colors simply by introducing a new color each time Row 15 and Row 1 are repeated.

Square 15: **Stepped Fret**

Colors A and C. Techniques: k, sl wyib, sl wyif
Multiple of 10 stitches

With A, cast on 43 stitches. Knit one row. Join C. Note: On all right-side rows, sl all sl-sts wyib. Always knit the last stitch of the row, which may come at any point in the line of directions.

SQUARE 15: *Stepped Fret*

Row 1 (right side)—With C, k1, * sl 1, (k1, sl 1) twice, k5; rep from *.

Row 2 and all other wrong-side rows—With the same color as previous row, knit all the same sts of that color again, and sl all the same sl-sts wyif.

Row 3—With A, k1, * k5, sl 1, k3, sl 1; rep from *.

Row 5—With C, k1, * sl 1, k1, sl 1, k3, (sl 1, k1) twice; rep from *.

Row 7—With A, k4, * (sl 1, k1) 3 times, sl 1, k3; rep from *.

Row 9—With C, k1, * sl 1, k5, sl 1, k3; rep from *.

Row 11—With A, k2, * (sl 1, k1) twice, sl 1, k5; rep from *.

Row 13—With C, knit.

Rows 15, 17, 19, 21, 23, and 25—Repeat Rows 11, 9, 7, 5, 3, and 1.

Row 27—With A, knit.

Row 28 (wrong side)—See Row 2.

Repeat Rows 1–28 three times (84 rows). Bind off on right side with A, knitting all stitches.

The Stepped Fret is a motif common in many forms of primitive art, often showing dark and light motifs interlocking, as in this pattern.

Square 16: **Double Scroll**

Colors B and C. Techniques: k, sl wyib, sl wyif
Multiple of 16 stitches

With B, cast on 43 stitches. Knit one row. Join C. Note: on all right-side rows, sl all sl-sts wyib. Always knit the last stitch of the row, which may come at any point in the line of directions.

Row 1 (right side)—With C, k1, sl 2, * k13, sl 3; rep from *.

Row 2 and all other wrong-side rows—With the same color as previous row, knit all the same sts of that color again, and sl all the same sl-sts wyif.

Row 3—With B, k3, * (sl 1, k1) 3 times, sl 1, k5, sl 1, k3; rep from *.
Row 5—With D, k2, * sl 1, k7, (sl 1, k3) twice; rep from *.
Row 7—With B, k1, * sl 1, k3, sl 1, k1, sl 1, k3, sl 3, k3; rep from *.
Row 9—With D, k4, * sl 1, k3, sl 1, k7, sl 1, k3; rep from *.
Row 11—With B, k3, * sl 1, k3, sl 1, k7, sl 1, k3; rep from *.
Row 13—With D, k2, * (sl 1, k3) twice, sl 3, k3, sl 1, k1; rep from *.
Row 15—With B, k5, * (sl 1, k3) twice, sl 1, k7; rep from *.

SQUARE 16: *Double Scroll*

Row 17—With D, k2, * sl 1, k1, sl 1, k3, sl 1, k5, (sl 1, k1) twice; rep from *.

Row 19—With B, k5, * sl 3, k13; rep from *.

Row 20 (wrong side)—See Row 2.

Repeat Rows 1–20 four times, then Rows 1 and 2 again (82 rows). With B, knit 2 rows; then bind off on right side, knitting all stitches.

In this interesting pattern you can see dark-colored "scrolls" moving upward to the left, and light-colored "scrolls" moving downward to the right, as the motifs interlock.

SECTION III—SLIP-STITCH PATTERNS

There are many other things that can be done with slip-stitches, in addition to using them as simple vertical pattern lines as Mosaic Patterns do. Slip-stitches need not always be slipped wyib on right-side rows and wyif on wrong-side rows. This can be reversed. Nor do they have to be slipped over only 2 rows. They can be slipped over 4, 6, or 8 rows, too. They can be elongated, moved over to the left or right, or stranded across the front of the fabric and caught up by a later row. The patterns in this section will show you some of the other design effects that slip-stitches can create.

In general, directions for slip-stitch patterns may look complicated at first. But they are usually patterns of the kind that make an orderly and obvious design, so the sequence is easily learned by working through the pattern rows once. You'll find these patterns interesting and fun to work, as they begin to give you a small hint of the endless variety of fabric designs that hand-knitting makes possible.

Square 17: **Woven Tweed**

Colors A and D. Techniques: k, p, sl wyif
Multiple: odd number of stitches

With A, cast on 45 stitches. Purl one row. Join D.
   Row 1 (right side)—With D, k1, * sl 1 wyif, k1; rep from *.

SQUARE 17: *Woven Tweed*

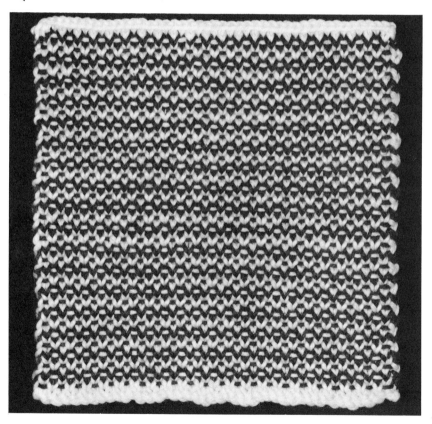

Row 2—With D, purl.

Row 3—With A, k2, * sl 1 wyif, k1; rep from *, end k1.

Row 4—With A, purl.

Repeat Rows 1–4 seventeen times (68 rows). Bind off on right side with A, knitting all stitches.

Woven stitches are those that are slipped while the yarn is carried across them on the right side of the work—that is, wyif on a right-side row, or wyib on a wrong-side row. Of course, when you are knitting on a right-side row after slipping a stitch wyif, it is necessary to pass the yarn between the needle points to the back again so it will be in position for knitting.

Notice the attractive wrong side of this simple tweed pattern, which shows little horizontal chains of the two colors.

Square 18: **Hexagon Pattern**

Colors B and D. Techniques: k, p, sl wyib, sl wyif
Multiple of 8 stitches plus 6

With D, cast on 38 stitches. Knit 2 rows. Join B.

Rows 1, 3, and 5 (right side)—With B, k2, * sl 2 wyib, k6; rep from *, end sl 2, k2.

Rows 2, 4, and 6—With B, p2, * sl 2 wyif, p6; rep from *, end sl 2, p2.

Rows 7, 8, 9 and 10—With D, knit.

Rows 11, 13, and 15—With B, k6, * sl 2 wyib, k6; rep from *.

Rows 12, 14, and 16—With B, p6, * sl 2 wyif, p6; rep from *.

Rows 17, 18, 19, and 20—With D, knit.

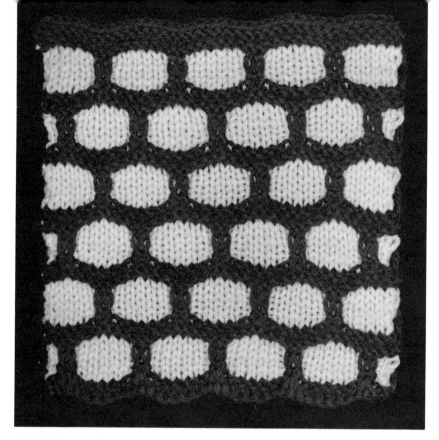

SQUARE 18: *Hexagon Pattern*

Repeat Rows 1–20 three times (60 rows). Bind off on right side with D, knitting all stitches.

This square shows how slip-stitches can draw horizontal rows out of line, upward and downward, when the same slip-stitches are carried over more than 2 rows. The Color D bands in this pattern are forced by the slip-stitches to zigzag up and down slightly, giving a somewhat hexagonal shape to the motifs.

Square 19: **Instant Plaid**

Colors A and C. Techniques: k, p, sl wyib, sl wyif, k wrapping twice, drop
Multiple of 8 stitches plus 6

With A, cast on 46 stitches. Knit one row. Join C.
Row 1 (right side)—With C, k1, * sl 1 wyib, k2, sl 1 wyib, k4; rep from *, end last repeat k1.

SQUARE 19: *Instant Plaid*

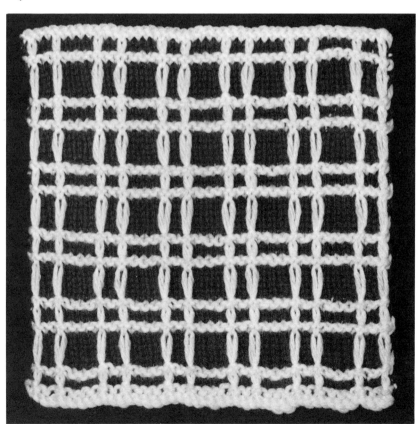

Row 2—With C, k1, * sl 1 wyif, p2, sl 1 wyif, p4; rep from *, end last repeat k1.

Row 3—With A, knit.

Row 4—With A, k1, * k1 wrapping twice, k2, k1 wrapping twice, k4; rep from *, end last repeat k1.

Row 5—With C, repeat Row 1, dropping extra wraps off needle when slipping sl-sts.

Rows 6, 8, and 10—Repeat Row 2.

Rows 7 and 9—Repeat Row 1.

Rows 11 and 12—With A, knit.

Repeat Rows 1–12 five times, then Rows 1–3 again (63 rows). Bind off on wrong side with A, knitting all stitches.

This pattern demonstrates the use of elongated stitches, formed by the extra wraps on Row 4, to extend upward over the following 6 rows.

Square 20: **Scale Quilting**

Colors B and D. Techniques: k, p, sl wyib, sl wyif
Multiple of 6 stitches plus 1

With D, cast on 43 stitches. Purl one row. Join B. Preparation row (right side)—With B, k1, sl 1 wyib, * k3, sl 3 wyib; rep from *, end k3, sl 1 wyib, k1.

Row 1 (wrong side)—With B, k1, sl 1 wyib, * p3, sl 3 wyib; rep from *, end p3, sl 1 wyib, k1.

Rows 2 and 4—With D, knit.

Rows 3 and 5—With D, purl.

Row 6—With B, k2, * sl 3 wyib, k1, insert needle from front under loose B strand of Row 1, and knit next st, k1; rep from *, end sl 3 wyib, k2.

Row 7—With B, k1, p1, * sl 3 wyib, p3; rep from *, end sl 3 wyib, p1, k1.

Rows 8, 9, 10, and 11—Repeat Rows 2, 3, 4, and 5.

Row 12—With B, k1, sl 1 wyib, * k1, insert needle from front under loose B strand of Row 7 and knit next st, k1, sl 3 wyib; rep from *, end last repeat sl 1 wyib, k1 instead of sl 3 wyib.

SQUARE 20: *Scale Quilting*

Repeat Rows 1–12 five times, then Rows 1–6 again (66 rows). Bind off on wrong side with B, purling all stitches.

This beautiful pattern illustrates the fact that when stitches are slipped wyib on wrong-side rows, the carried strands naturally appear on the right side of the work. Of course, when you are purling after slipping stitches wyib, the yarn must be brought forward between the needle points to return to the purl position for the next stitch.

SQUARE 21: *Florentine Frieze*

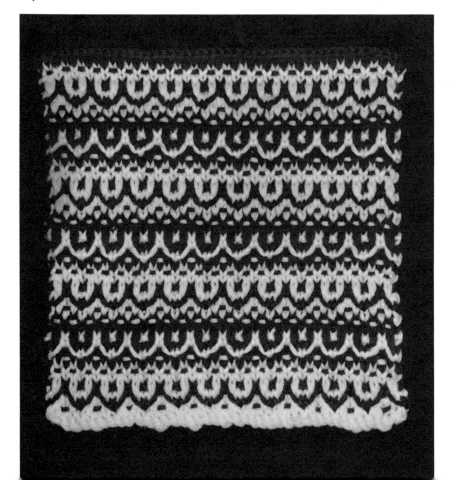

Square 21: **Florentine Frieze**

Colors A and D. Techniques: k, p, sl wyib, sl wyif
Multiple of 4 stitches plus 1

With A, cast on 45 stitches. Purl one row. Join D.

Row 1 (right side)—With D, k1, * sl 1 wyib, sl 1 wyif, sl 1 wyib, k1;
   rep from *.

Row 2—With D, p1, * sl 3 wyib, p1; rep from *.

Row 3—With A, knit.

Row 4—With A, purl.

Row 5—With D, k1, * sl 1 wyib, insert needle from front under loose
   D strand of Row 2 and knit next st, sl 1 wyib, k1; rep from *.

Row 6—With D, k1, * sl 1 wyif, p1, sl 1 wyif, k1; rep from *.

Rows 7 and 8—Repeat Rows 3 and 4.

Row 9—With D, k1, * sl 1 wyif, k1; rep from *.

Row 10—With D, purl.

Rows 11 through 20—Repeat Rows 1 through 10, *reversing colors.*

Repeat Rows 1–20 three times, then Rows 1–10 again (70 rows). Bind
off on right side with D, knitting all stitches.

Florentine Frieze is a handsome pattern for sweaters. It looks pretty
when worked in more than two colors, by changing to a new color on
each first and eleventh row.

Square 22: **Diagonal Weave**

Colors B and C. Techniques: k, p, sl wyib, sl wyif, drop
Multiple of 4 stitches plus 3

With B, cast on 47 stitches. Purl one row. Join C.
    Row 1 (right side)—With C, k2, * sl 1 wyib, k3; rep from *, end k1.
    Row 2—With C, p4, * sl 1 wyif, p3; rep from *, end last repeat p2.

SQUARE 22: *Diagonal Weave*

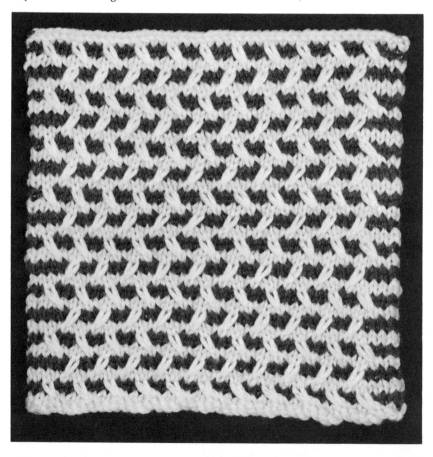

Row 3—With B, k2, * drop sl-st off needle, k2, pick up dropped st, place on left-hand needle and knit it; k1; rep from *, end k1.

Row 4—With B, purl.

Row 5—With C, k6, * sl 1 wyib, k3; rep from *, end k1.

Row 6—With C, p4, * sl 1 wyif, p3; rep from *, end p3.

Row 7—With B, k4, * sl 2 wyib, drop sl-st off needle, sl same 2 sts back to left-hand needle, pick up dropped st, place on left-hand needle and knit it; k3; rep from *, end k3.

Row 8—With B, purl.

Repeat Rows 1–8 seven times, then Rows 1–3 again (59 rows). Bind off on wrong side with B, purling all stitches.

This handsome pattern demonstrates that slip-stitches (made on Rows 1, 2, 5, and 6 in this case) may be moved over, a couple of stitches to the left or to the right, when they are being picked up for re-knitting. The technique is not difficult, and it does create some striking effects.

Square 23: **Honeycomb**

Colors A and C. Techniques: k, p, sl wyib, sl wyif, drop
Multiple of 6 stitches plus 4

With A, cast on 46 stitches.

Row 1 (wrong side)—With A, k4, * p2, k4; rep from *. (Join C)

Rows 2 and 4—With C, k4, * sl 2 wyib, k4; rep from *.

Rows 3 and 5—With C, k4, * sl 2 wyif, k4; rep from *.

Row 6—With A, k1, * sl 2 wyib, k4; rep from *, end sl 2, k1.

Row 7—With A, k1, * sl 2 wyif, k1, p2, k1; rep from *, end sl 2, k1.

Rows 8 through 11—Repeat Rows 2 through 5.

Row 12—With A, k2, * sl 2 wyib, drop Color A sl-st off needle, sl

SQUARE 23: *Honeycomb*

same 2 sts back to left-hand needle, pick up dropped st, place on
left-hand needle and knit it; k2, drop Color A sl-st off needle, k2,
pick up dropped st, place on left-hand needle and knit it; rep from
*, end k2.

Row 13—With A, k2, p1, * k4, p2; rep from *, end k4, p1, k2.

Rows 14 and 16—With C, k2, sl 1 wyib, * k4, sl 2 wyib; rep from *,
end k4, sl 1, k2.

Rows 15 and 17—With C, k2, sl 1 wyif, * k4, sl 2 wyif; rep from *, end k4, sl 1, k2.

Row 18—With A, k4, * sl 2 wyib, k4; rep from *.

Row 19—With A, k2, p1, * k1, sl 2 wyif, k1, p2; rep from *, end k1, sl 2, k1, p1, k2.

Rows 20 through 23—Repeat Rows 14 through 17.

Row 24—With A, k2, * drop Color A sl-st off needle, k2, pick up dropped st, place on left-hand needle and knit it; sl 2 wyib, drop Color A sl-st off needle, sl same 2 sts back to left-hand needle, pick up dropped st, place on left-hand needle and knit it, k2; rep from *, end k2.

Repeat Rows 1–24 three times, then Rows 1–12 again (84 rows). Bind off on wrong side with A, knitting all stitches.

This is one of many Honeycombs, an especially firm, close one that makes nice jackets, pillows and hats.

Square 24: **Cottage Check**

Colors A and D. Techniques: k, p, sl wyib, sl wyif
Multiple of 4 stitches plus 3

Special note: this pattern must be worked back and forth on a circular needle or a pair of double-pointed needles. At the end of every row marked "turn," turn the work around as usual. At the end of every row marked "slide," slide the stitches to the other end of the needle, without turning the work, so that the same side is still facing.

With A, cast on 43 stitches. Purl one row. Join D.

Row 1 (right side)—With D, k2, * sl 1 wyib, k1; rep from *, end k1. Slide.

SQUARE 24: *Cottage Check*

Row 2—With A, k1, * sl 1 wyib, k1; rep from *. Turn.

Row 3—With D, p2, * sl 1 wyif, p3; rep from *, end p1. Slide.

Row 4—With A, p4, * sl 1 wyif, p3; rep from *, end sl 1, p2. Turn.

Row 5—With D, k1, * sl 1 wyib, k1; rep from *. Slide.

Row 6—With A, k4, * sl 1 wyib, k3; rep from *, end sl 1, k2. Turn.

Row 7—With D, p4, * sl 1 wyif, p3; rep from *, end sl 1, p2. Slide.

Row 8—With A, p1, * sl 1 wyif, p1; rep from *. Turn.

Row 9—With D, repeat Row 1. Slide.

Row 10—With A, knit. Turn.

Row 11—With D, p1, * sl 1 wyif, p1; rep from *. Slide.

Row 12—With A, purl. Turn.

Repeat Rows 1–12 five times, then Rows 1–6 again (66 rows). Bind off on wrong side with A, purling all stitches.

This square demonstrates a class of patterns in which one strand of color chases the other strand in the same direction, so there are 2 right-side rows at once, then 2 wrong-side rows, etc. In this case the first of each pair of rows is worked with D, the second with A, so the turns come only after A rows. Naturally one cannot work this way on single-pointed needles, so it must be done on a circular needle or a pair of dpn's. If you are using a pair of short (7") dpn's, be sure to keep the knitting fairly well bunched together, so it does not slip off the opposite end of the needle while you are working.

SECTION IV—TWIST-STITCH PATTERNS

If you are a beginner, you can use this section to make the first creative decisions of your knitting career: the decisions about which version of the right-side Left Twist and Right Twist you are going to adopt. The Glossary gives two ways of doing each. For most patterns, either way is good; for some patterns, one way is a trifle better than the other; in the majority of cases, the choice is entirely up to you, depending on which way comes more easily to you and feels more comfortable. Certainly you should know both versions of a right-side Left Twist and both versions of a right-side Right Twist, so try them out thoroughly and study them to see which you prefer. It won't harm a pattern square to have one version of each twist worked in some of its rows, and the other version of each twist worked in other rows. The difference is negligible, and the practice is valuable.

There are also wrong-side versions of the Left Twist and Right Twist (only one of each), which you should know even though they are generally used in a smaller number of patterns than the right-side versions. Basically, *any* twist is done by skipping the first stitch on the left needle and working the second stitch before it, then working the first stitch afterward. The different versions are concerned only with whether the two stitches are worked together or not worked together.

Twist-stitch patterns are related to cable patterns, in that their effects depend on moving stitches diagonally. to the right or left. But twist stitches usually move only one stitch over one stitch at a time, while cables can move larger numbers of stitches at once. This section and the following one will demonstrate this very clearly.

Square 25: **Wave**

Color A. Techniques: k, p, RT, LT
Multiple of 9 stitches plus 8

Cast on 44 stitches.
Row 1 (wrong side) and all other wrong-side rows—Purl.
Row 2—P2, * k4, LT, p3; rep from *, end k4, p2.
Row 4—P2, * k4, p1, LT, p2; rep from *, end k4, p2.
Row 6—P2, * k4, p2, LT, p1; rep from *, end k4, p2.

(Opposite) SQUARE 25: *Wave*

SQUARE 26: *Twisted Columns*

Row 8—P2, * k4, p3, LT; rep from *, end k4, p2.
Row 10—P2, k4, * p4, k5; rep from *, end p2.
Row 12—P2, * k4, p3, RT; rep from *, end k4, p2.
Row 14—P2, * k4, p2, RT, p1; rep from *, end k4, p2.
Row 16—P2, * k4, p1, RT, p2; rep from *, end k4, p2.
Row 18—P2, * k4, RT, p3; rep from *, end k4, p2.
Row 20—P2, * k5, p4; rep from *, end k4, p2.

Repeat Rows 1–20 twice, then Rows 1–18 again (58 rows). Bind off on wrong side, purling all stitches.

This is a good-looking, easy and useful pattern for all kinds of garments, which also lends itself to panel formation when worked in a single repeat.

Square 26: **Twisted Columns**

Colors B and C. Techniques: k, p, sl wyib, sl wyif, RT, LT
Multiple of 10 stitches plus 4

With B, cast on 44 stitches. Knit one row. Join C.
Row 1 (right side)—With C, k1, * sl 2 wyib, k3; rep from *, end sl 2, k1.
Row 2—With C, k1, * sl 2 wyif, k3; rep from *, end sl 2, k1.
Row 3—With B, k1, * RT, k3, LT, k3; rep from *, end RT, k1.
Row 4—With B, k1, * p2, k3; rep from *, end p2, k1.

Repeat Rows 1–4 twenty times (80 rows). Bind off on right side with B, knitting all stitches.

This easy-to-work pattern makes a thick, cosy fabric for coats, jackets, pillows and blankets. The background stripes (Rows 1 and 2) may be worked in many different colors instead of just one second color.

Square 27: **Wickerwork**

Color A. Techniques: k, p, RT, LT
Multiple of 8 stitches

Cast on 48 stitches.
Row 1 (wrong side)—P1, * k2, p2; rep from *, end k2, p1.
Row 2—* K1, p1, RT, LT, p1, k1; rep from *.
Row 3—* P1, k1, p1, k2, p1, k1, p1; rep from *.

SQUARE 27: *Wickerwork*

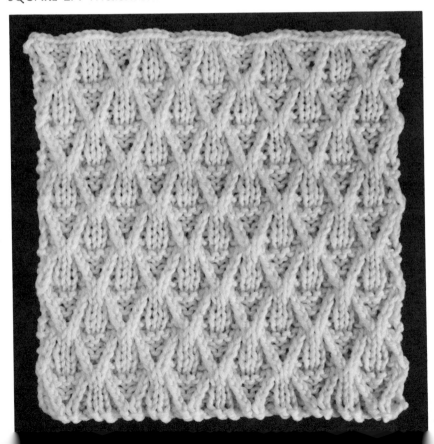

Row 4—* K1, RT, p2, LT, k1; rep from *.

Row 5—P2, * k4, p4; rep from *, end k4, p2.

Row 6— Knit.

Row 7—Repeat Row 1.

Row 8—* LT, p1, k2, p1, RT; rep from *.

Row 9—* K1, p1, k1, p2, k1, p1, k1; rep from *.

Row 10—* P1, LT, k2, RT, p1; rep from *.

Row 11—K2, * p4, k4; rep from *, end p4, k2.

Row 12—Knit.

Repeat Rows 1–12 four times, then Rows 1–5 again (53 rows). Bind off on right side, knitting all stitches.

This easy pattern shows one of the pretty fabric textures that knit, purl and twist stitches can make.

Square 28: **Twining Rib Pattern**

Color B. Techniques: k, p, RT, LT
Multiple of 6 stitches

Cast on 48 stitches.

Rows 1 and 3 (wrong side)—K2, * p2, k4; rep from *, end p2, k2.

Row 2—K2, * RT, p4; rep from *, end RT, k2.

Row 4—K4, * p4, k2; rep from *, end k2.

Rows 5 through 11—Repeat Rows 1 through 4, then Rows 1, 2, and 3 again.

Row 12—K3, * LT, p2, RT; rep from *, end k3.

Row 13—K2, p1, k1, * p1, k2; rep from *, end p1, k1, p1, k2.

Row 14—K3, p1, * LT, RT, p2; rep from *, end LT, RT, p1, k3.

Rows 15 and 17—K2, p1, k2, * p2, k4; rep from *, end p2, k2, p1, k2.

Row 16—K3, p2, * LT, p4; rep from *, end LT, p2, k3.

Row 18—K3, p1, * RT, LT, p2; rep from *, end RT, LT, p1, k3.
Row 19—Repeat Row 13.
Row 20—K3, * RT, p2, LT; rep from *, end k3.

Repeat Rows 1–20 twice, then Rows 1–11 again (51 rows). Bind off on right side, knitting over knit stitches and purling over purl stitches.

The first 4 rows of this pattern, if repeated over and over, will make a typical Twisted or Baby Cable ribbing. Such ribs may also be worked closer together, with only 2 or 3 purl stitches between them instead of 4.

SQUARE 28: *Twining Rib Pattern*

Square 29: **Leaning Stripes**

Colors B and D. Techniques: k, p, sl wyib, sl wyif, RT
Multiple of 3 stitches

With B, cast on 54 stitches. Purl one row. Join D.
    Row 1 (right side)—With D, k1, * RT, sl 1 wyib; rep from *, end k2.
    Row 2—With D, * p2, sl 1 wyif; rep from *, end p3.
    Row 3—With B, k1, * sl 1 wyib, RT; rep from *, end sl 1, k1.

SQUARE 29: *Leaning Stripes*

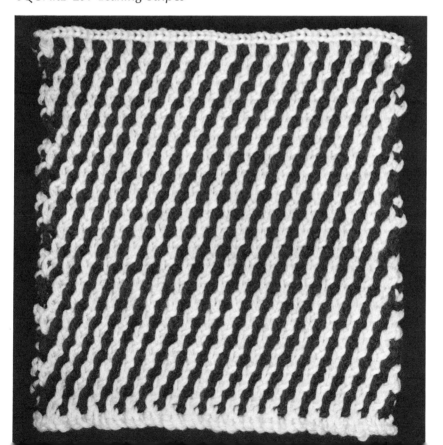

Row 4—With B, p1, * sl 1 wyif, p2; rep from *, end sl 1, p1.
Row 5—With D, * RT, sl 1 wyib; rep from *, end RT, k1.
Row 6—With D, p3, * sl 1 wyif, p2; rep from *.
Rows 7 through 12—Repeat Rows 1 through 6, *reversing colors.*

Repeat Rows 1–12 six times, then Rows 1–10 again (82 rows). Bind off on right side with B, knitting all stitches.

This striped fabric is very dense, as you can tell by the relatively large number of stitches required to make the square; so it is good for knitting warm and windproof garments.

Square 30: **Twisted Lattice**

Color B. Techniques: k, p, RT, LT
Multiple of 12 stitches plus 10

Cast on 46 stitches.
Row 1 (wrong side) and all other wrong-side rows—Purl.
Row 2—P1, k3, * RT, k10; rep from *, end RT, k3, p1.
Row 4—P1, k2, * RT, LT, k8; rep from *, end RT, LT, k2, p1.
Row 6—P1, k1, * RT, k2, LT, k6; rep from *, end RT, k2, LT, k1, p1.
Row 8—P1, * RT, k4, LT, k4; rep from *, end RT, k4, LT, p1.
Row 10—P1, k7, * LT, k2, RT, k6; rep from *, end k1, p1.
Row 12—P1, k8, * LT, RT, k8; rep from *, end p1.
Row 14—P1, k9, * LT, k10; rep from *, end LT, k9, p1.
Row 16—P1, k8, * RT, LT, k8; rep from *, end p1.
Row 18—P1, k7, * RT, k2, LT, k6; rep from *, end k1, p1.
Row 20—P1, * LT, k4, RT, k4; rep from *, end LT, k4, RT, p1.
Row 22—P1, k1, * LT, k2, RT, k6; rep from *, end LT, k2, RT, k1, p1.
Row 24—P1, k2, * LT, RT, k8; rep from *, end LT, RT, k2, p1.

SQUARE 30: *Twisted Lattice*

Repeat Rows 1–24 twice, then Rows 1–6 again (54 rows). Bind off on wrong side, purling all stitches.

This is the classic Lattice, with simple, clear diagonal lines that add interest to any knitted garment. Variations in the multiple will make the diamond shapes larger or smaller, the twisted ribs closer or farther apart. The background may be purl, garter or seed stitches as well as knit stitches.

Square 31: **Twisted Panels**

Color B. Techniques: k, p, k-b, RT, LT
Panels of 5, 6, and 10 stitches

Cast on 48 stitches.

Rows 1 and 3 (wrong side)—K1, p1, k2, p5, k3, p5, k2, p10, k2, p5, k3, p5, k2, p1, k1.

SQUARE 31: *Twisted Panels*

Row 2—K1, k1-b, p2, LT, k3, p3, LT, k3, p2, k3, RT, LT, k3, p2, k3, RT, p3, k3, RT, p2, k1-b, k1.

Row 4—K1, k1-b, p2, k1, LT, k2, p2, RT, LT, RT, p2, k2, RT, k2, LT, k2, p2, LT, RT, LT, p2, k2, RT, k1, p2, k1-b, k1.

Rows 5 and 7—K1, p1, (k2, p5) twice, k3, p10, k3, (p5, k2) twice, p1, k1.

Row 6—K1, k1-b, p2, k2, LT, k1, p2, k3, RT, p3, k1, RT, k4, LT, k1, p3, LT, k3, p2, k1, RT, k2, p2, k1-b, k1.

Row 8—K1, k1-b, p2, k3, LT, p2, LT, RT, LT, p2, RT, k6, LT, p2, RT, LT, RT, p2, RT, k3, p2, k1-b, k1.

Repeat Rows 1–8 six times, then Rows 1–6 again (54 rows). Bind off on wrong side, knitting over knit stitches and purling over purl stitches.

Three kinds of decorative panels are shown in this square: one a braid, one with diagonal stripes and one with V shapes like a Double Cable. Notice that the arrangement of panels is symmetrical in relation to the center, the patterns being worked in opposite ways on the left and right. Even the braids are worked in opposition, one beginning with a twist to the left, the other with a twist to the right. Remember this when you plan a garment or some other project displaying a series of panels. Symmetrical arrangement of designs on each side of a common center gives balance and unity to the finished article.

Square 32: **Assorted Mock Cables**

Color B. Techniques: k, p, k-b, RT, LT, PRT, PLT, Tw 3
Panels of 2, 3, and 6 stitches

Cast on 51 stitches.

Row 1 (wrong side)—K1, p1, (k3, p2) twice, k3, (PRT) 3 times, k3, p3, k3, (PLT) 3 times, k3, (p2, k3) twice, p1, k1.

Row 2—K1, k1-b, p3, LT, p3, k2, p3, k6, p3, k3, p3, k6, p3, k2, p3, RT, p3, k1-b, k1.

Row 3—K1, p1, k3, p2, k3, PRT, k3, p1, (PRT) twice, p1, k3, p3, k3, p1, (PLT) twice, p1, k3, PLT, k3, p2, k3, p1, k1.

Row 4—K1, k1-b, (p3, k2) twice, p3, k6, p3, Tw 3, p3, k6, p3, (k2, p3) twice, k1-b, k1.

SQUARE 32: *Assorted Mock Cables*

Repeat Rows 1–4 twelve times, then Rows 1–3 again (51 rows). Bind off on right side, knitting over knit stitches and purling over purl stitches.

In this square, 7 decorative ribs demonstrate 5 kinds of twists, 3 worked from the right side and 2 from the wrong side, giving you a good opportunity to compare them. Such decorative ribs look attractive when worked in combination with cables and other patterns.

SECTION V—CABLES

Cables are among the most fascinating of knitting patterns. They can be panel or all-over designs, and can produce hundreds of varying types of fabrics. The basic principle of cabling is very simple. It's just a matter of moving some stitches diagonally across other stitches. The cable needle (dpn) is used to hold one group of stitches while the other group is being worked.

The stitches in front of the crossing, showing on the right side of the fabric, are cable stitches. The stitches in back of the crossing, behind and hidden by the cable stitches, are background stitches. If the background stitches are worked first, while the dpn holds the cable stitches in front, the result is a Front Cross: the cable stitches travel to the left. If the cable stitches are worked first, while the dpn holds the background stitches in back, the result is a Back Cross: the cable stitches travel to the right. Grasp this simple principle, and you will always understand the mechanism of any cable pattern.

Cable stitches are usually knitted on the right side and purled on the wrong side, because a vertical rib worked like this will stand out in relief on the surface of the fabric. Background stitches may be either knitted or purled on the right side. A plain purl background occurs frequently in cable patterns, because it tends to retreat, thus displaying the knit ribs to best advantage. Cables worked in panel arrangements have purl stitches between them, to make the knit ribs stand out.

Instructions for cable crossings almost always tell you to "hold" the dpn with its stitches in front or in back while working the other stitches. But this doesn't mean that you literally have to hold onto it. You just let go of it and let it hang there. After all, you need both hands to work the other stitches and you can't spare any extra fingers to grip the dpn, until you are ready to pick it up again and work the stitches from it. Don't be afraid that the dpn will slide out of the stitches in the meantime. To make it do this, you'd have to really try.

Remember also that when you *slip* stitches to the dpn, you always slip them *purlwise,* as when slipping stitches in any other pattern, so the right-hand sides of the loops will be forward. When working the stitches off the dpn, hold it and use it as if it were an extra left-hand needle.

Square 33: **Simple Cables with Moss Stitch**

Color B. Techniques: k, p, k-b, p-b, BC, FC
Panel of 12 stitches for each cable

Cast on 47 stitches.

Row 1 (right side)—(K1, p1) 5 times, (k1-b, p3, k6, p3) twice, k1-b, (p1, k1) 5 times.

Row 2—(P1, k1) 5 times, p1-b, (k3, p6, k3, p1-b) twice, (k1, p1) 5 times.

Row 3—(P1, k1) 5 times, (k1-b, p3, k6, p3) twice, k1-b, (k1, p1) 5 times.

SQUARE 33: *Simple Cables with Moss Stitch*

Row 4—(K1, p1) 5 times, p1-b, (k3, p6, k3, p1-b) twice, (p1, k1) 5 times.

Row 5—(K1, p1) 5 times, k1-b, p3, sl next 3 sts to dpn and hold in back, k3, then k3 from dpn (BC made); p3, k1-b, p3, sl next 3 sts to dpn and hold in front, k3, then k3 from dpn (FC made); p3, k1-b, (p1, k1) 5 times.

Rows 6, 7, and 8—Repeat Rows 2, 3, and 4.

Repeat Rows 1–8 six times, then Rows 1–5 again (53 rows). Bind off on wrong side, knitting over knit stitches and purling over purl stitches.

Notice that the cable made with back crosses (BC) twists to the right, while the cable made with front crosses (FC) twists to the left. When Simple Cable panels are used in a garment on each side of a common center, they should be worked in opposition, like this, for better symmetry.

Moss Stitch, which forms the side panels in this square, is another classic non-curling knit-purl fabric. Like its close relative, Seed Stitch, it is often used for borders and for filling between panels of other patterns such as cables.

Square 34: **Double Cables**

Color B. Techniques: k, p, k-b, p-b, BC, FC
Panel of 16 stitches for each cable

Cast on 56 stitches.
Notes: *FC (front cross)*—sl 3 sts to dpn and hold in front, k3, then k3 from dpn.

  BC (back cross)—sl 3 sts to dpn and hold in back, k3, then k3 from dpn.

Row 1 (wrong side) and all other wrong-side rows—K2, (p1-b, k2, p12, k2) 3 times, p1-b, k2.
Row 2—K2, k1-b, (p2, k12, p2, k1-b) 3 times, k2.
Row 4—K2, k1-b, p2, BC, FC, p2, k1-b, (p2, FC, BC, p2, k1-b) twice, k2.
Rows 6, 8, and 10—Repeat Row 2.

Row 12—K2, k1-b, (p2, BC, FC, p2, k1-b) twice, p2, FC, BC, p2, k1-b, k2.

Rows 14 and 16—Repeat Row 2.

Repeat Rows 1–16 three times, then Rows 1–5 again (53 rows). Bind off on right side, knitting over knit stitches and purling over purl stitches.

SQUARE 34: *Double Cables*

The center panel of this square shows one version of the Chain or Medallion cable; the other two panels show the typical Double or Horseshoe cable, one opening away from its center and the other closing toward its center. Varying numbers of stitches and pattern rows make varying sizes and styles of the basic Double Cable.

Square 35: **Lacing Cable**

Color B. Techniques: k, p, k-b, FC, BC, FPC, BPC
Panel of 24 stitches

Cast on 48 stitches.
Notes: FC *(front cross)*—sl 3 sts to dpn and hold in front, k3, then k3 from dpn.

BC *(back cross)*—sl 3 sts to dpn and hold in back, k3, then k3 from dpn.

FPC *(front purl cross)*—sl 3 sts to dpn and hold in front, p2, then k3 from dpn.

BPC *(back purl cross)*—sl 2 sts to dpn and hold in back, k3, then p2 from dpn.

Rows 1 and 3 (wrong side)—P15, k6, p6, k6, p15.
Row 2—K14, k1-b, p6, BC, p6, k1-b, k14.
Row 4—K14, k1-b, p4, BPC, FPC, p4, k1-b, k14.
Row 5—P15, (k4, p3) twice, k4, p15.
Row 6—K12, FPC, BPC, p4, FPC, BPC, k12.
Rows 7, 9, 11, 13, and 15—P12, k2, p6, k8, p6, k2, p12.
Rows 8 and 14—K11, k1-b, p2, FC, p8, FC, p2, k1-b, k11.
Rows 10 and 12—K11, k1-b, p2, k6, p8, k6, p2, k1-b, k11.
Row 16—K12, BPC, FPC, p4, BPC, FPC, k12.

SQUARE 35: *Lacing Cable*

Row 17—Repeat Row 5.
Row 18—K14, k1-b, p4, FPC, BPC, p4, k1-b, k14.

Repeat Rows 1–18 three times (54 rows). Bind off on wrong side, knitting over knit stitches and purling over purl stitches.

The Lacing Cable is very striking when inserted, as here, into a Stockinette Stitch fabric. Variations include: 2-stitch ribs instead of 3-stitch ribs; diagonal movement on the background 1 stitch at a time instead of 2 stitches at a time; or extra cable rows to make another twist in the center.

Square 36: **Arches**

Color A. Techniques: k, p, FC, BC
Multiple of 12 stitches plus 2

Cast on 50 stitches.
Notes: *FC (front cross)*—sl 2 sts to dpn and hold in front, k2, then k2 from dpn.
BC (back cross)—sl 2 sts to dpn and hold in back, k2, then k2 from dpn.

Row 1 (wrong side) and all other wrong-side rows—K1, p48, k1.
Row 2—Knit.
Row 4—K1, * BC, k4, FC; rep from *, end k1.
Row 6—Knit.
Row 8—K3, * FC, BC, k4; rep from *, end last repeat k3.

Repeat Rows 1–8 seven times (56 rows). Bind off on wrong side, purling all stitches.

This square shows one example of a class of patterns in which cable crossings are embedded in a Stockinette Stitch fabric. Such patterns are usually simple to work, and give very nice texture effects.

(Opposite) SQUARE 36: *Arches*

Square 37: **Wrung-Rib Pattern**

Color B. Techniques: k, p, FC, BC
Multiple of 12 stitches plus 7

Cast on 55 stitches.
Notes: *FC (front cross)*—sl 4 sts to dpn and hold in front, k3, sl central
purl st from dpn back to left-hand needle and purl it, then k3
from dpn.
BC (back cross)—sl 4 sts to dpn and hold in back, k3, sl central
purl st from dpn back to left-hand needle and purl it, then k3
from dpn.

Rows 1 and 3 (right side)—K1, p2, * k3, p1, k3, p5; rep from *, end k4.
Rows 2, 4, 6, and 8—K1, p3, * k5, p3, k1, p3; rep from *, end k3.
Row 5—K1, p2, * FC, p5; rep from *, end k4.
Row 7—Repeat Row 1.
Rows 9 and 11—K4, * p5, k3, p1, k3; rep from *, end p2, k1.
Rows 10, 12, 14, and 16—K3, * p3, k1, p3, k5; rep from *, end p3, k1.
Row 13—K4, * p5, BC; rep from *, end p2, k1.
Row 15—Repeat Row 9.

Repeat Rows 1–16 three times, then Rows 1–6 again (54 rows). Bind
off on right side, knitting over knit stitches and purling over purl
stitches.

This interesting pattern demonstrates the cabling technique used to
make a crossing of an odd number of stitches, when the central stitch
is to be placed between the two groups on either side. The central

(Opposite) SQUARE 37: *Wrung-Rib Pattern*

stitch in these cables is a purl stitch, which helps to distinguish it from the knit groups that cross in front and in back of it. In other such patterns, the central stitch may be a knit stitch like all the others in the cable.

Square 38: **Open Cables and Four-Rib Braid**

Color B. Techniques: k, p, k-b, FC, BC, FPC, BPC
Panels of 15 and 18 stitches

Cast on 54 stitches.

Notes: *FC (front cross)*—sl 3 sts to dpn and hold in front, k3, then k3 from dpn.

BC (back cross)—sl 3 sts to dpn and hold in back, k3, then k3 from dpn.

FPC (front purl cross)—sl 3 sts to dpn and hold in front, p1, then k3 from dpn.

BPC (back purl cross)—sl 1 st to dpn and hold in back, k3, then p1 from dpn.

Row 1 (wrong side)—K2, p1, k6, p6, k6, p12, k6, p6, k6, p1, k2.
Row 2—K2, k1-b, p6, FC, p6, k3, FC, k3, p6, BC, p6, k1-b, k2.
Row 3 and all subsequent wrong-side rows—K2, knit all knit sts and purl all purl sts across row to last 2 sts, k2.
Row 4—K2, k1-b, p5, BPC, FPC, p5, k12, p5, BPC, FPC, p5, k1-b, k2.
Row 6—K2, k1-b, p4, BPC, p2, FPC, p4, (BC) twice, p4, BPC, p2, FPC, p4, k1-b, k2.
Row 8—K2, k1-b, p3, BPC, p4, FPC, p3, k12, p3, BPC, p4, FPC, p3, k1-b, k2.

Row 10—K2, k1-b, p3, k3, p6, k3, p3, k3, FC, k3, p3, k3, p6, k3, p3, k1-b, k2.

Row 12—K2, k1-b, p3, FPC, p4, BPC, p3, k12, p3, FPC, p4, BPC, p3, k1-b, k2.

Row 14—K2, k1-b, p4, FPC, p2, BPC, p4, (BC) twice, p4, FPC, p2, BPC, p4, k1-b, k2.

Row 16—K2, k1-b, p5, FPC, BPC, p5, k12, p5, FPC, BPC, p5, k1-b, k2.

SQUARE 38: *Open Cables and Four-Rib Braid*

Repeat Rows 1–16 three times, then Rows 1–10 again (58 rows). Bind off on wrong side, knitting over knit stitches and purling over purl stitches.

Two Open Cables appear in this square, one crossing to the right and the other to the left. These cables are often used on button bands, since buttonholes can be attractively placed in their open centers. The Four-Rib Braid in the middle of the square is one of dozens of different versions of a braided cable, which may have 3, 4, 5 or more ribs with varying numbers of stitches in each rib.

Square 39: **Cabled Lattice**

Color A. Techniques: k, p, FC, BC, FPC, BPC
Multiple of 10 stitches plus 2

Cast on 52 stitches.
Notes: *FC (front cross)*—sl 2 sts to dpn and hold in front, k2, then k2 from dpn.

BC *(back cross)*—sl 2 sts to dpn and hold in back, k2, then k2 from dpn.

FPC (front purl cross)—sl 2 sts to dpn and hold in front, p1, then k2 from dpn.

BPC (back purl cross)—sl 1 st to dpn and hold in back, k2, then p1 from dpn.

Row 1 (wrong side)—(P1, k1) twice, * p4, k6; rep from *, end p4, (k1, p1) twice.
Row 2—(P1, k1) twice, * FC, p6; rep from *, end FC, (k1, p1) twice.
Row 3 and all subsequent wrong-side rows—Knit all knit sts and purl all purl sts.

SQUARE 39: *Cabled Lattice*

Row 4—K1, p1, k1, * BPC, FPC, p4; rep from *, end BPC, FPC, k1, p1, k1.

Row 6—P1, k1, * BPC, p2, FPC, p2; rep from *, end last repeat k1, p1 instead of p2.

Row 8—K1, * BPC, p4, FPC; rep from *, end k1.

Row 10—P1, k2, * p6, BC; rep from *, end p6, k2, p1.

Row 12—K1, * FPC, p4, BPC; rep from *, end k1.

Row 14—P1, k1, * FPC, p2, BPC, p2; rep from *, end last repeat k1, p1 instead of p2.

Row 16—K1, p1, k1, * FPC, BPC, p4; rep from *, end FPC, BPC, k1, p1, k1.

Repeat Rows 1–16 three times, then Rows 1–8 again (56 rows). Bind off on wrong side, knitting over knit stitches and purling over purl stitches.

This Cabled Lattice is one of many versions. In other versions the ribs of the lattice may be wider or narrower; they may be closer together or farther apart; the background may be worked in purl stitches, as here, or in Seed Stitch or Moss Stitch or some other fabric; it may have secondary patterns such as diamonds, ribs or bobbles.

Square 40: **Variation Cables**

Color B. Techniques: k, p, k-b, b-p, and Variation Cable Crossings (see Notes)
Panels of 6 and 9 stitches

Cast on 58 stitches.

Notes: *Ribbed Cable Front Cross*—sl 5 sts to dpn and hold in front, (k1-b, p1) twice, then from dpn (k1-b, p1) twice, k1-b.

Ribbed Cable Back Cross—sl 4 sts to dpn and hold in back, (k1-b, p1) twice, k1-b, then from dpn (p1, k1-b) twice.

End-Over-End Front Cross—sl 6 sts to dpn and hold in front, twist dpn ½ turn clockwise, k6 from dpn.

End-Over-End Back Cross—sl 6 sts to dpn and hold in front, twist dpn ½ turn counterclockwise, k6 from dpn.

Gordian Knot—sl 4 sts to dpn and hold in front, k2, then sl the 2 purl sts from dpn back to left-hand needle, then pass dpn with 2 remaining knit sts to back of work; p2 from left-hand needle, k2 from dpn.

Row 1 (wrong side) and all other wrong-side rows—K1, p1, k3, (p1-b, k1) 4 times, p1-b, k3, p6, k3, p2, k2, p2, k3, p6, k3, p1-b, (k1, p1-b) 4 times, k3, p1, k1.
Row 2—K1, k1-b, p3, (k1-b, p1) 4 times, k1-b, p3, k6, p3, k2, p2, k2, p3, k6, p3, k1-b, (p1, k1-b) 4 times, p3, k1-b, k1.

SQUARE 40: *Variation Cables*

Row 4—K1, k1-b, p3, Ribbed Cable Front Cross, p3, End-Over-End
   Front Cross, p3, Gordian Knot, p3, End-Over-End Back Cross, p3,
   Ribbed Cable Back Cross, p3, k1-b, k1.
Rows 6, 8, and 10—Repeat Row 2.

Repeat Rows 1–10 five times, then Rows 1–5 again (55 rows). Bind
off on right side, knitting over knit stitches and purling over purl
stitches.

These patterns demonstrate some unusual ways of handling the cable
needle, which may come as a surprise even to knitters who have done
a lot of cable work. The End-Over-End Cable, which looks almost—
but not quite—like an ordinary Simple Cable, is especially interesting,
and its cross is certainly faster to work than the usual cable cross. The
Ribbed Cable changes knit stitches to purl stitches, and vice versa, on
the group of stitches that passes in back of the cross. It also exemplifies
the principle of the uneven cable, in which a greater number of stitches
cross in front than behind.

SECTION VI—INCREASE-AND-DECREASE PATTERNS

This is probably the most important section in this book, for no knitter
can be a good knitter without a precise understanding of increases
and decreases. They are what create shaping, both in fabric patterns
and in garment proportions. The most detailed material in the Glossary
concerns increases and decreases, and it's necessary for you to compre-
hend all of it. These patterns will help you do so.

In particular, be aware of how decreases are often paired—for instance, a "k2 tog" at one side of a motif matched by a "ssk" at the
other side. This is essential to the symmetry of increase-and-decrease

patterns and of lace patterns. The decreases are more than methods of reducing the number of stitches; they are integral elements of the design. They are used in the same way, in symmetrical pairs, to shape garments. Learn to recognize the left or right slant and the general appearance of every kind of decrease. This knowledge will stand you in good stead later.

Directions for some of these pattern squares are rather lengthy, but that doesn't mean that they are difficult to work. It only means that it's usually necessary to write out every row of an increase-and-decrease pattern, simply because stitch counts may be different on every row. Read the directions carefully and methodically as you go along, and you'll find the patterns easy to understand as well as interesting to knit.

Square 41: **Bias Stripes**

Colors B and D. Techniques: k, inc, k2 tog, k2 tog-b, sl 1—k2 tog— psso
Multiple: odd number of stitches

With B, cast on 3 stitches. Knit one row. Join D. With D, knit one row, turn, (inc) twice, k1, making 5 stitches. Now work Increase Rows as follows:

Row 1 (right side)—With B, knit.
Row 2—With B, k1, inc, knit to last 2 sts, inc, k1.
Rows 3 and 4—With D, repeat Rows 1 and 2.

Repeat these 4 rows until there are 28 2-row stripes, 57 stitches on needle. With B, knit 2 rows even. Then work Decrease Rows as follows:

Row 1 (right side)—With D, k1, k2 tog, knit to last 3 sts, k2 tog-b, k1.
Row 2—With D, knit.
Rows 3 and 4—With B, repeat Rows 1 and 2.

SQUARE 41: *Bias Stripes*

Repeat these 4 rows until 5 stitches remain. With D, k2 tog, k1, k2 tog-b, turn, k3. Break D. With B, k3, turn, sl 1—k2 tog—psso. Break B, leaving a 3″ end. Draw yarn-end through last stitch and fasten off on wrong side.

Bias knitting may be used with any sort of pattern. Bias squares worked in mosaic patterns, for example, make interesting pillows and bags; bias strips make attractive neckties, scarves and stoles. Whole garments can be shaped with bias knitting. The principle is always the same: beginning at one corner, single increases are made every other row on both sides until one edge is the desired width; then, to maintain the bias, one side is decreased, the other continues to increase, to the desired length; then both sides are decreased for a straight edge at the top. Any kind of single increases or single decreases may be used.

Square 42: **Ripple**

Colors B and C. Techniques: k, p, sl 2—k1—p2sso, double inc, ssk, k2 tog
Multiple of 10 stitches plus 5

With B, cast on 45 stitches. Purl one row. Join C.
Row 1 (right side)—With C, k2, ssk, * k3, double inc, k3, sl 2—k1—p2sso; rep from *, end k3, double inc, k3, k2 tog, k2.
Row 2—With C, k2, purl across to last 2 sts, k2.
Rows 3 and 4—With B, repeat Rows 1 and 2.

Repeat these 4 rows until there are 12 stripes of Color C and 12 stripes of Color B counting the first wrong-side purl row. With B, work one more right-side row, then bind off on wrong side, purling all stitches.

Ripple knitting is almost a separate technique in itself. The basic increase-and-decrease pattern can be varied with any sort of color combination and with wrong-side rows either knitted or purled, or some of each; and the number of stitches to a repeat may be different. You could have, for instance, 4 stitches between the double increases and the double decreases (a multiple of 12), or 5 stitches (a multiple of 14), or 6 stitches (a multiple of 16), etc.; you could even have some repeats wider than others in the same piece.

Patterns of this type cause the cast-on and bound-off edges to form scallops. You may think that this is going to create a bit of a problem in joining this "square" into your afghan—and you're right. But don't worry. It can be flattened out well enough, and after all your Learn-To-Knit sampler wouldn't be complete without a basic Ripple.

SQUARE 42: *Ripple*

Square 43: **Trinity Stitch**

Color A. Techniques: p, (k1, p1, k1), p3 tog
Multiple of 4 stitches

Cast on 48 stitches.
Rows 1 and 3 (right side)—Purl.
Row 2—* (K1, p1, k1) in one stitch, p3 tog; rep from *.
Row 4—* P3 tog, (k1, p1, k1) in one stitch; rep from *.

SQUARE 43: *Trinity Stitch*

Repeat Rows 1–4 fourteen times (56 rows). Bind off on right side, purling all stitches.

Trinity Stitch, also known as Cluster Stitch, Bramble Stitch, Blackberry Stitch and several other names, is a classic Aran texture pattern often used along with cables in fisherman sweaters. It makes interesting panels in otherwise plain garments, and has become one of the most popular of the "nubby" increase-and-decrease patterns.

Square 44: **Cocoon Stitch**

Color B. Techniques: k, p, k-b, k under running thread, (k1, yo, k1),
p5 tog
Multiple of 8 stitches plus 3

Cast on 51 stitches.
Row 1 (wrong side)—K1, p1, * k1, p1, k5, p1; rep from *, end k1.
Row 2—K1, k1-b, * p5, k1-b, p1, k1-b; rep from *, end k1.
Row 3—K1, p1, * k1 under running thread, (k1, yo, k1) in next st, k1 under running thread, p1, p5 tog, p1; rep from *, end k1.
Rows 4, 6, and 8—K1, k1-b, * p1, k1-b, p5, k1-b; rep from *, end k1.
Rows 5 and 7—K1, p1, * k5, p1, k1, p1; rep from *, end k1.
Row 9—K1, p1, * p5 tog, p1, k1 under running thread, (k1, yo, k1) in next st, k1 under running thread, p1; rep from *, end k1.
Rows 10, 11, and 12—Repeat Row 2, Row 1, and Row 2 again.

Repeat Rows 1–12 four times, then Rows 1–11 again (59 rows). Bind

(Opposite) SQUARE 44: *Cocoon Stitch*

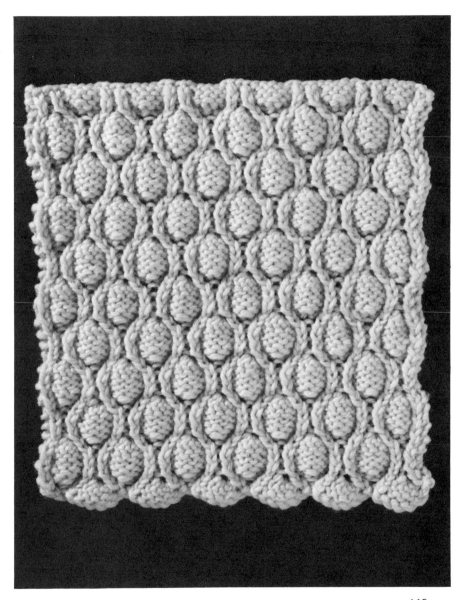

off on right side, knitting over knit stitches and purling over purl stitches.

Although the knit ribs in this handsome texture pattern are worked straight up, notice how the 5-stitch increases and decreases draw them into graceful curves framing the purled "cocoons."

Square 45: **Bobble and Leaf**

Color A. Techniques: k, p, k-b, p-b, k2 tog, ssk, sl 1—k2 tog—psso, p3 tog, (k1, yo, k1), (k1, yo, k1, yo, k1), MB, turn
Multiple of 14 stitches plus 7

Cast on 49 stitches. Note: MB (make bobble) as follows: (k1, yo, k1, yo, k1) in one stitch, turn, p5, turn, k5, turn, p1, p3 tog, p1, turn, sl 1—k2 tog—psso, completing bobble.

Rows 1 and 3 (wrong side)—P2, k3, * p7, k7; rep from *, end p2.

Row 2—P1, k1-b, * p7, k7; rep from *, end p3, k1-b, p1.

Row 4—P1, k1-b, p3, * MB, p3, ssk, k3, k2 tog, p3; rep from *, end k1-b, p1.

Row 5—P2, k3, * p5, k3, p1-b, k3; rep from *, end p2.

Row 6—P1, k1-b, p3, * (k1, yo, k1) in next st, p3, ssk, k1, k2 tog, p3; rep from *, end k1-b, p1.

Row 7—P2, k3, * p3, k3; rep from *, end p2.

Row 8—P1, k1-b, p3, * k1, (k1, yo, k1) in next st, k1, p3, sl 1—k2 tog —psso, p3; rep from *, end k1-b, p1.

Row 9—P2, * k7, p5; rep from *, end k3, p2.

Row 10—P1, k1-b, p3, * k2, (k1, yo, k1) in next st, k2, p7; rep from *, end k1-b, p1.

Rows 11 and 13—P2, * k7, p7; rep from *, end k3, p2.

Row 12—P1, k1-b, p3, * k7, p7; rep from *, end k1-b, p1.

Row 14—P1, k1-b, p3, * ssk, k3, k2 tog, p3, MB, p3; rep from *, end k1-b, p1.

Row 15—P2, k3, * p1-b, k3, p5, k3; rep from *, end p2.

Row 16—P1, k1-b, p3, * ssk, k1, k2 tog, p3, (k1, yo, k1) in next st, p3; rep from *, end k1-b, p1.

Row 17—Repeat Row 7.

Row 18—P1, k1-b, p3, * sl 1—k2 tog—psso, p3, k1, (k1, yo, k1) in next st, k1, p3; rep from *, end k1-b, p1.

SQUARE 45: *Bobble and Leaf*

Row 19—P2, k3, * p5, k7; rep from *, end p2.

Row 20—P1, k1-b, * p7, k2, (k1, yo, k1) in next st, k2; rep from *, end p3, k1-b, p1.

Repeat Rows 1–20 twice, then Rows 1–12 again (52 rows). Bind off on wrong side, knitting over knit stitches and purling over purl stitches.

This square demonstrates two popular increase-and-decrease formations: the bobble, which is worked by increasing in one stitch and making several short rows over the increased stitches before decreasing; and the embossed leaf, which is worked by increasing at one spot throughout several rows, then decreasing throughout several more. Both formations have many variations. A bobble, requiring only one stitch and one row for its completion, can be placed anywhere. It is often used as a decoration for cable patterns. The embossed leaf can be used in panels or in border bands, as well as all over the fabric.

Not all of the rows in this pattern maintain the same number of stitches. You'll find that Rows 5 through 9 and 15 through 19 have 2 stitches less per repeat, reducing the multiple to 12. This is not at all uncommon in increase-and-decrease patterns; in fact, it is more usual than not. If you should want to start or stop such a pattern on one of its off-count rows, you must take into consideration this kind of a change in multiple.

Square 46: **Reverse Fern Stitch**

Color A. Techniques: k, p, k-b, k2 tog, ssk, inc, double inc
Multiple of 12 stitches plus 3

Cast on 51 stitches.

Row 1 (wrong side)—Purl.

Row 2—P1, * k1-b, p4, k3, p4; rep from *, end k1-b, p1.

SQUARE 46: *Reverse Fern Stitch*

Row 3—P2, * k4, p3, k4, p1; rep from *, end p1.

Row 4—P1, * k1-b, p3, k2 tog, double inc, ssk, p3; rep from *, end k1-b, p1.

Row 5—P2, * k3, p5, k3, p1; rep from *, end p1.

Row 6—P1, * k1-b, p2, k2 tog, k1, double inc, k1, ssk, p2; rep from *, end k1-b, p1.

Row 7—P2, * k2, p7, k2, p1; rep from *, end p1.

Row 8—P1, * k1-b, p1, k2 tog, k2, double inc, k2, ssk, p1; rep from *, end k1-b, p1.

Row 9—P2, * k1, p9, k1, p1; rep from *, end p1.

Row 10—P1, * k1-b, k2 tog, k3, double inc, k3, ssk; rep from *, end k1-b, p1.

Row 11—Purl.

Row 12—P1, k2, * p4, k1-b, p4, k3; rep from *, end last repeat k2, p1 instead of k3.

Row 13—P3, * k4, p1, k4, p3; rep from *.

Row 14—P1, inc, * ssk, p3, k1-b, p3, k2 tog, double inc; rep from *, end last repeat inc, p1 instead of double inc.

Row 15—P4, * k3, p1, k3, p5; rep from *, end last repeat p4.

Row 16—P1, inc, * k1, ssk, p2, k1-b, p2, k2 tog, k1, double inc; rep from *, end last repeat inc, p1 instead of double inc.

Row 17—P5, * k2, p1, k2, p7; rep from *, end last repeat p5.

Row 18—P1, inc, * k2, ssk, p1, k1-b, p1, k2 tog, k2, double inc; rep from *, end last repeat inc, p1 instead of double inc.

Row 19—P6, * k1, p1, k1, p9; rep from *, end last repeat p6.

Row 20—P1, inc, * k3, ssk, k1-b, k2 tog, k3, double inc; rep from *, end last repeat inc, p1 instead of double inc.

Repeat Rows 1–20 twice, then Rows 1–16 again (56 rows). Bind off on wrong side, knitting over knit stitches and purling over purl stitches.

Double increases arranged in a continuous vertical line, as shown in the lower half of each diamond-shaped motif in this pattern, make the best kind of shaping for the raglan "seams" of a seamless sweater yoke worked from the neck down. There are at least a dozen different methods for shaping such a raglan yoke with different kinds of increases, but this pattern, showing stitches fanning out from the increase lines, gives you the basic idea.

Square 47: **Inchworm**

Colors B and C. Techniques: k, p, sl wyib, sl wyif, k2 tog, ssk, p2 tog,
*   p2 tog-b, (k1, yo, k1, yo, k1, yo, k1)*
Multiple of 10 stitches

With C, cast on 40 stitches. Purl one row. Join B.
    Row 1 (right side)—With B, * k2, (k1, yo, k1, yo, k1, yo, k1) in one st,

SQUARE 47: *Inchworm*

making 7 sts from 1; k2, sl 2 wyib, k1, sl 2 wyib; rep from *, end last repeat sl 1 wyib, k1 instead of sl 2 wyib.

Row 2—With B, k1, sl 1 wyif, * k1, sl 2 wyif, k11, sl 2 wyif; rep from *, end k1, sl 2 wyif, k11.

Row 3—With C, k1, * k2 tog, k5, ssk, k7; rep from *, end last repeat k6.

Row 4—With C, p6, * p2 tog-b, p1, sl 1 wyif, p1, p2 tog, p7; rep from *, end last repeat p1.

Row 5—With C, k1, * k2 tog, sl 1 wyib, ssk, k7; rep from *, end last repeat k6.

Row 6—With C, purl.

Row 7—With B, k1, sl 1 wyib, * k1, sl 2 wyib, k2, (k1, yo, k1, yo, k1, yo, k1) in one st, k2, sl 2 wyib; rep from *, omit final "sl 2 wyib" from last repeat.

Row 8—With B, * k11, sl 2 wyif, k1, sl 2 wyif; rep from *, end last repeat sl 1 wyif, k1 instead of sl 2 wyif.

Row 9—With C, k6, * k2 tog, k5, ssk, k7; rep from *, end last repeat k1.

Row 10—With C, p1, * p2 tog-b, p1, sl 1 wyif, p1, p2 tog, p7; rep from *, end last repeat p6.

Row 11—With C, k6, * k2 tog, sl 1 wyib, ssk, k7; rep from *, end last repeat k1.

Row 12—With C, purl.

Repeat Rows 1–12 five times (60 rows). Bind off on right side with C, knitting all stitches.

This is a good example of the type of pattern that increases a lot of stitches all at once, then gradually decreases them away on subsequent rows.

Square 48: **Vine Leaf Panel**

Color A. Techniques: k, p, k-b, inc, purl inc, (k1, yo, k1), M1, k2
tog, ssk, sl 1—k2 tog—psso, p2 tog
Panel of 26 stitches

Cast on 9 stitches, place a marker on needle, cast on 26 stitches, place another marker on needle, cast on 9 stitches—44 stitches total.

SQUARE 48: *Vine Leaf Panel*

Row 1 (wrong side)—P9, sl marker, k5, p5, k4, p3, k9, sl marker, p9.

Row 2—K8, k1-b, sl marker, p7, p2 tog, inc, k2, p4, k2, (k1, yo, k1) in next st, k2, p5, sl marker, k1-b, k8.

Throughout subsequent rows, continue to work the first and last 9 stitches in Stockinette Stitch, slipping markers, as established in these 2 rows; continue the center panel between markers as follows:

Row 3—K5, p7, k4, p2, k1, p1, k8.

Row 4—P6, p2 tog, k1-b, purl inc, k2, p4, k3, (k1, yo, k1) in next st, k3, p5.

Row 5—K5, p9, k4, p2, k2, p1, k7.

Row 6—P5, p2 tog, k1-b, purl inc, p1, k2, p4, ssk, k5, k2 tog, p5.

Row 7—K5, p7, k4, p2, k3, p1, k6.

Row 8—P4, p2 tog, k1-b, purl inc, p2, k2, p4, ssk, k3, k2 tog, p5.

Row 9—K5, p5, k4, p2, k4, p1, k5.

Row 10—P5, (k1, yo, k1) in next st, p4, k2, p4, ssk, k1, k2 tog, p5.

Row 11—K5, p3, k4, p2, k4, p3, k5.

Row 12—P5, k1, (k1, yo, k1) in next st, k1, p4, k1, M1, k1, p2 tog, p2, sl 1—k2 tog—psso, p5.

Row 13—K9, p3, k4, p5, k5.

Row 14—P5, k2, (k1, yo, k1) in next st, k2, p4, k1, inc, k1-b, p2 tog, p7.

Row 15—K8, p1, k1, p2, k4, p7, k5.

Row 16—P5, k3, (k1, yo, k1) in next st, k3, p4, k2, purl inc, k1-b, p2 tog, p6.

Row 17—K7, p1, k2, p2, k4, p9, k5.

Row 18—P5, ssk, k5, k2 tog, p4, k2, p1, purl inc, k1-b, p2 tog, p5.

Row 19—K6, p1, k3, p2, k4, p7, k5.

Row 20—P5, ssk, k3, k2 tog, p4, k2, p2, purl inc, k1-b, p2 tog, p4.

Row 21—K5, p1, k4, p2, k4, p5, k5.

Row 22—P5, ssk, k1, k2 tog, p4, k2, p4, (k1, yo, k1) in next st, p5.

Row 23—K5, p3, k4, p2, k4, p3, k5.

Row 24—P5, sl 1—k2 tog—psso, p2, p2 tog, k1, M1, k1, p4, k1, (k1, yo, k1) in next st, k1, p5.

Repeat Rows 1–24 twice, then Rows 1–6 again (54 rows). Bind off on wrong side, knitting over knit stitches and purling over purl stitches.

This beautiful increase-and-decrease panel makes a striking decoration for a sweater front or sleeve, and you can place it anywhere, just by setting two markers 26 stitches apart as shown in this square. Notice that the Stockinette edge stitches that adjoin the panel are knitted in back every right-side row, as directed in Row 2. This is a designer's trick to prevent these stitches from becoming too loose, as they are sometimes inclined to do when placed next to purl stitches in this way. It's worth remembering for your future projects.

SECTION VII—LACE

There are so many hundreds of beautiful lace patterns in knitting that it's hard to choose just a few for a little sampling like this one. The selections have been made with the object of providing practice in as many different lace-knitting techniques as possible.

Knitted lace is prettiest when worked with fine yarn on small needles. But as the squares in this section amply prove, it also gives very nice effects with worsted-weight yarn on medium-sized needles. Almost any lace pattern may be used to make lovely scarves, shawls, overskirts, stoles, summer sweaters and baby things.

When you are working lace, remember to cast on and bind off *loosely*, and stretch each lace pattern when blocking or pressing, to open up the holes. Because lace stretches so readily, most of the squares in this section have fewer stitches and rows than those in other sections. The holes allow these patterns to spread to more width and height than other types of patterns. Therefore, with lace, a greater area can be covered with less knitting.

All lace patterns are actually increase-and-decrease patterns, of a special kind. Every yarn-over is an increase. It makes a hole; and it also places a new stitch on the needle. Therefore in every lace pattern there are decreases to compensate for the increases created by the yarn-overs, and to maintain the same number of stitches. One single decrease compensates for one single yarn-over, or one double decrease compensates for two single yarn-overs at once. Similarly, a double yarn-over is compensated for by two single decreases or one double decrease. As you work these patterns you will perceive various ways of matching yarn-overs and decreases, which illustrate the basic principles of lace knitting.

Square 49: **Tilted Trellis**

Color A. Techniques: k, p, yo, k2 tog, ssk
Multiple of 16 stitches plus 3

Cast on 35 stitches.
  Row 1 (wrong side) and all other wrong-side rows—K1, p33, k1.
  Rows 2, 4, 6, and 8—K1, * (ssk, yo) 4 times, k8; rep from *, end k2.
  Rows 10, 12, 14, and 16—K2, * k8, (yo, k2 tog) 4 times; rep from *, end k1.

Repeat Rows 1–16 three times, then Rows 1–4 again (52 rows). Bind off *loosely* on right side, knitting all stitches.

The Trellis formation—a yarn-over and single decrease—made every right-side row—is the basic constituent of most lace patterns. There are two general types of Trellis, one in which the decrease comes before the yarn-over, and the other in which it comes after. The first half of this pattern shows the former, the second half the latter.

This square demonstrates the fact that when the same kind of Trellis is worked *in the same spot* for several consecutive rows, it draws the fabric into a bias slant. Notice the blocks of plain Stockinette Stitch here, in which the stitches lie at two different angles instead of running

SQUARE 49: *Tilted Trellis*

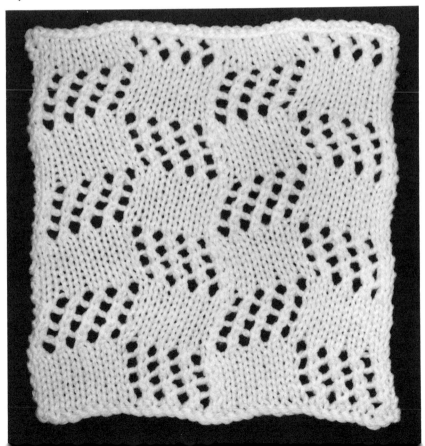

straight up. This tilted effect is created by alternating the two different types of bias Trellis.

When the Trellis is moved one stitch over to the right or left every other pattern row, the bias is eliminated. This will be shown by other lace patterns.

Square 50: **Arrowhead Mesh**

Color A. Techniques: k, p, yo, k2 tog, ssk, k3 tog, sl 1—k2 tog—psso
Multiple of 10 stitches plus 3

Cast on 33 stitches.
Rows 1 and 3 (wrong side)—K1, p31, k1.
Row 2—K2, * (yo, ssk) twice, yo, k3 tog, yo, k2 tog, yo, k1; rep from *, end k1.
Row 4—K3, * yo, ssk, yo, sl 1—k2 tog—psso, yo, k2 tog, yo, k3; rep from *.

Repeat Rows 1–4 thirteen times (52 rows). Bind off *loosely* on wrong side, purling all stitches.

In this pattern the two types of Trellis are shown alternating in panels without bias, because the yarn-over-and-decrease units are moved one stitch over, every other pattern row. The left-slanting and right-slanting decreases are placed in opposition to each other, which gives a herring-bone effect. Observe the formation of this lace very closely as you work it, because many other lace patterns make use of the same principles.

(Opposite) SQUARE 50: *Arrowhead Mesh*

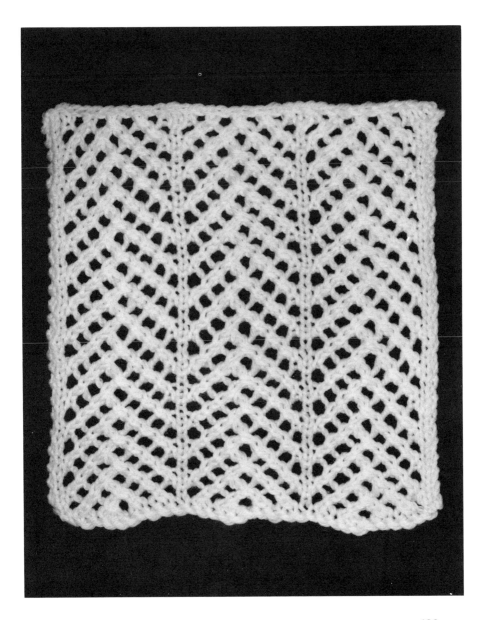

Square 51: **Faggoting and Fancy Rib**

*Color A. Techniques: k, p, yo, ssk, p2 tog, sl 1—k1—psso, sl 1—k2
    tog—psso*
Multiple of 8 stitches

Cast on 32 stitches.
  Row 1 (wrong side) and all other wrong-side rows—P2, * p2 tog, yo,
  p6; rep from *, end last repeat p4.

SQUARE 51: *Faggoting and Fancy Rib*

Row 2—P2, * sl 1—k1—psso, yo, k2, yo, ssk, k2; rep from *, end sl 1—k1—psso, yo, k2, p2.

Row 4—P2, * sl 1—k1—psso, yo, k3, yo, ssk, k1; rep from *, end sl 1—k1—psso, yo, k2, p2.

Row 6—P2, * sl 1—k1—psso, yo, k4, yo, ssk; rep from *, end sl 1—k1—psso, yo, k2, p2.

Row 8—P2, sl 1—k1—psso, * yo, k5, yo, sl 1—k2 tog—psso; rep from *, end yo, k2, p2.

Repeat Rows 1–8 six times, then Row 1 again (49 rows). Bind off *loosely* on right side, purling all stitches.

Faggoting is a basic lace stitch, typically exhibiting panels of zigzag openwork. It is nearly always constructed of yarn-overs and decreases worked on both right-side and wrong-side rows. It is used in borders, decorative insertions and lacy articles such as scarves.

Square 52: **Lace Diamonds**

Color A. Techniques: k, p, yo, k2 tog, ssk, sl 1—k2 tog—psso
Multiple of 8 stitches plus 3

Cast on 35 stitches.

Row 1 (wrong side) and all other wrong-side rows—Purl.

Row 2—P1, k1, * yo, ssk, k3, k2 tog, yo, k1; rep from *, end p1.

Row 4—P1, k2, * yo, ssk, k1, k2 tog, yo, k3; rep from *, end last repeat k2, p1 instead of k3.

Row 6—P1, k3, * yo, sl 1—k2 tog—psso, yo, k5; rep from *, end last repeat k3, p1 instead of k5.

Row 8—P1, k2, * k2 tog, yo, k1, yo, ssk, k3; rep from *, end last repeat k2, p1 instead of k3.

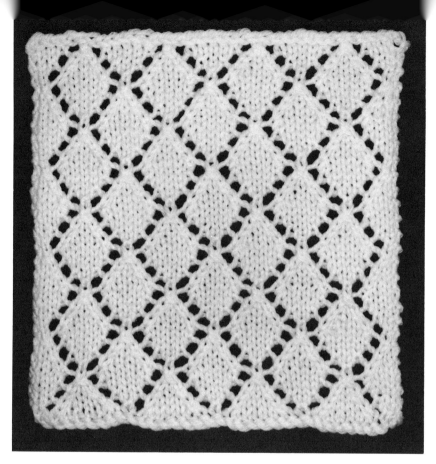

SQUARE 52: *Lace Diamonds*

Row 10—P1, k1, * k2 tog, yo, k3, yo, ssk, k1; rep from *, end p1.
Row 12—P1, k2 tog, * yo, k5, yo, sl 1—k2 tog—psso; rep from *, end
    last repeat ssk, p1 instead of sl 1—k2 tog—psso.

Repeat Rows 1–12 four times, then Rows 1–6 again (54 rows). Bind
off *loosely* on wrong side, purling all stitches.

Innumerable variations on the Lace Diamonds pattern exist; some have diamonds of different sizes, some have decreases centered instead of placed at the sides of the diamonds, some have more or less openwork placed between diamonds, some have certain pattern rows repeated several times together. This version is one of the simplest and most basic of all, showing the diagonal lines of yarn-overs and paired decreases without embellishments.

Square 53: **Bumblebee Pattern**

Color A. Techniques: k, p, yo, ssk, k2 tog, yo2
Multiple of 8 stitches plus 4

Cast on 36 stitches.

Row 1 (wrong side) and all other wrong-side rows—Purl, always working (p1, k1) into the double loop of a yo2 made on a previous row.

Row 2—P1, k3, * k2 tog, yo2, ssk, k4; rep from *, end k2 tog, yo2, ssk, k3, p1.

Row 4—P1, * k2, k2 tog, k1, yo2, k1, ssk; rep from *, end k2, p1.

Row 6—P1, k1, * k2 tog, k2, yo2, k2, ssk; rep from *, end k1, p1.

Row 8—P1, k1, yo, * ssk, k4, k2 tog, yo2; rep from *, end ssk, k4, k2 tog, yo, k1, p1.

Row 10—P1, k1, yo, * k1, ssk, k2, k2 tog, k1, yo2; rep from *, end k1, ssk, k2, k2 tog, k1, yo, k1, p1.

Row 12—P1, k1, yo, * k2, ssk, k2 tog, k2, yo2; rep from *, end k2, ssk, k2 tog, k2, yo, k1, p1.

Repeat Rows 1–12 four times, then Row 1 again (49 rows). Bind off *loosely* on right side, purling all stitches.

SQUARE 53: *Bumblebee Pattern*

When purling wrong-side rows throughout this pattern, be sure to work 2 stitches into the long loops of the double yarn-overs, but only one stitch into the single yarn-overs made in the edge stitches on Rows 8, 10, and 12, so that the total number of stitches on the needle remains always the same.

Square 54: **Seafoam Pattern**

Colors A and C. Techniques: k, yo2, yo3, yo4, drop
Multiple of 10 stitches plus 6

With C, cast on 36 stitches. Knit one row. Join A.
  Row 1 (right side)—With A, k6, * yo2, k1, yo3, k1, yo4, k1, yo3, k1,
    yo2, k6; rep from *.

SQUARE 54: *Seafoam Pattern*

Row 2—With A, knit, dropping all yo's off needle.

Rows 3 and 4—With C, knit.

Row 5—K1, * yo2, k1, yo3, k1, yo4, k1, yo3, k1, yo2, k6; rep from *, end last repeat k1.

Row 6—With A, knit, dropping all yo's off needle.

Rows 7 and 8—With C, knit.

Repeat Rows 1–8 four times (32 rows). Bind off on right side with C, knitting all stitches.

Believe it or not, this lacy pattern is really nothing but Striped Garter Stitch—with multiple yarn-overs added to elongate some of the stitches and make the stripes wave up and down. This makes a light, fluffy fabric that is ideal for shawls, baby blankets, scarves and stoles.

Square 55: **Single-Strand Lace**

Color A. Techniques: k, p, yo, k2 tog, ssk, p2 tog, p2 tog-b, sl 1—k2 tog—psso, p3 tog-b

Multiple of 10 stitches plus 7

Cast on 37 stitches. Purl one row.

Row 1 (right side)—P1, k7, * yo, ssk, k8; rep from *, end yo, ssk, k6, p1.

Row 2—P6, * p2 tog-b, yo, p1, yo, p2 tog, p5; rep from *, end p1.

Row 3—P1, k4, * k2 tog, yo, k3, yo, ssk, k3; rep from *, end k1, p1.

Row 4—P4, * p2 tog-b, yo, p5, yo, p2 tog, p1; rep from *, end p3.

Row 5—P1, k1, * yo, sl 1—k2 tog—psso, yo, k7; rep from *, end last repeat k1, p1 instead of k7.

Row 6—P2, * p2 tog-b, yo, p8; rep from *, end last repeat p3.

SQUARE 55: *Single-Strand Lace*

Row 7—P1, * k2 tog, yo, k1, yo, ssk, k5; rep from *, end last repeat p1 instead of k5.

Row 8—P5, * yo, p2 tog, p3, p2 tog-b, yo, p3; rep from *, end p2.

Row 9—P1, k5, * yo, ssk, k1, k2 tog, yo, k5; rep from *, end p1.

Row 10—P7, * yo, p3 tog-b, yo, p7; rep from *.

Repeat Rows 1–10 four times, then Rows 1–5 again (45 rows). Bind off *loosely* on wrong side, purling all stitches.

Compare this pattern with Lace Diamonds. Notice that the yo holes here are divided from one another by a single strand of yarn, while in Lace Diamonds, and many other lace patterns, they are divided by two twisted strands. Single-Strand Lace like this is worked by making yarn-overs and decreases on *both* right-side and wrong-side rows, instead of on right-side rows only.

Remember that, should you find the "p3 tog-b" in Row 10 awkward to work, you can do it more easily by purling 2 stitches together, re-turning the resulting stitch to the left-hand needle, then passing the *next* stitch over the p2-tog stitch and off needle. Slip the stitch back to right-hand needle and proceed. This is really just a way of working "sl 1—k2 tog—psso" backward from the wrong side.

Square 56: **Elkhorn and Fleurette Panels**

Color A. Techniques: k, p, k-b, yo, yo2, k2 tog, ssk, k3 tog, k3 tog-b,
    sl 1—k2 tog—psso
Panels of 12 and 7 stitches

Cast on 34 stitches.
   Row 1 (wrong side) and all other wrong-side rows—K1, purl across to
      last stitch, k1. Always work (k1, p1) into the double loop of the
      yo2 made on Rows 2 and 4.
   Row 2—K4, yo, ssk, k1, k2 tog, (yo, k2, ssk) twice, yo2, (k2 tog, k2,
      yo) twice, ssk, k1, k2 tog, yo, k4.
   Row 4—K5, yo, k3, yo, k5, k3 tog, yo, k1-b, yo2, k1-b, yo, k3 tog-b,
      k5, yo, k3, yo, k5.
   Row 6—K3, k2 tog, yo, k2 tog, k1, ssk, yo, ssk, k2, (k2 tog, yo) twice,
      k2-b, (yo, ssk) twice, k2, k2 tog, yo, k2 tog, k1, ssk, yo, ssk, k3.

Row 8—K4, k2 tog, yo, k1, yo, ssk, k2, (k2 tog, yo) twice, k4, (yo, ssk) twice, k2, k2 tog, yo, k1, yo, ssk, k4.

Row 10—K5, (yo, k3) twice, (ssk, yo) twice, k4, (yo, k2 tog) twice, (k3, yo) twice, k5.

Row 12—K4, ssk, yo, sl 1—k2 tog—psso, yo, k2 tog, k2, (ssk, yo) twice, k4, (yo, k2 tog) twice, k2, ssk, yo, sl 1—k2 tog—psso, yo, k2 tog, k4.

SQUARE 56: *Elkhorn and Fleurette Panels*

Repeat Rows 1–12 four times, then Row 1 again (49 rows). Bind off *loosely* on right side, knitting all stitches.

Lace patterns can be used in panel combinations just like cables. Here is a panel of Elkhorn lace, flanked by two panels of Fleurette. Notice that 4 extra stitches are added to the square on Rows 4 and 10, as these rows contain 4 yarn-overs without compensating decreases. The extra stitches are removed on the following rows, each of which has 4 more decreases than yarn-overs.

You can insert a panel of lace in any plain Stockinette Stitch fabric, simply by placing 2 markers on the needle and working the lace pattern between them.

SECTION VIII—SPECIAL TECHNIQUES

In this section you'll find a few "different" pattern operations, and some knitting skills that you'll need to know when you make garments and other articles—such as picking up stitches, working short rows and shaping pieces in seamless circular knitting. This is a brief survey, designed to prepare you to grasp any sort of knitting directions quickly and easily, and to show you that the basic language of knitting can be written to describe many kinds of things to be done with yarn and needles.

If you've been making your afghan squares in numerical order, you are now within 7 squares of finishing the course and earning your P.G.K. (Pretty Good Knitter) degree. After that, you can tackle just about anything. Continue your knitting education on your own, always trying new patterns and meeting new challenges that will add to your store of knowledge; for this is the fastest—and perhaps the only—route to mastery of the craft.

What will your next project be?

Square 57: **Star Stitch**

Colors B and C. Techniques: k, p, yo, pass
Multiple of 3 stitches

With B, cast on 33 stitches.

Rows 1 and 3 (wrong side)—With B, purl.

Row 2—With B, k2, * yo, k3, then with point of left-hand needle pass 3rd st on right-hand needle over the first and 2nd sts, and off needle; rep from *, end k1.

Row 4—With B, k1, * k3, pass 3rd st on right-hand needle over first and 2nd sts and off needle, yo; rep from *, end k2. (Join C.)

Rows 5 and 6—With C, repeat Rows 1 and 2.

Rows 7 and 8—With B, repeat Rows 3 and 4.

Rows 9 and 10—With B, repeat Rows 1 and 2.

Rows 11 and 12—With C, repeat Rows 3 and 4.

Repeat Rows 1–12 four times, then Rows 1–4 again (52 rows). Bind off *loosely* on wrong side with B, purling all stitches.

This interesting pattern has several unusual characteristics. For one thing, it changes colors at the left-hand edge instead of the right-hand edge; for another, it passes a knit stitch over 2 other stitches instead of a slip-stitch, as is more usual. The use of different colors in the pattern is optional. Colors may be changed every other row throughout (Rows 1 and 2 with B, Rows 3 and 4 with C), which gives a very different

SQUARE 57: *Star Stitch*

effect. Try it, and if you like it, make the square that way. Or, the pattern may be worked in many colors, one or two stripes of each at a time; or it may be worked in one single color. It makes a delicate, lacy fabric that stretches readily.

146

Square 58: **Blister Stitch**

Colors A and C. Techniques: k, p, drop
Multiple of 4 stitches plus 3

With C, cast on 35 stitches.
  Row 1 (wrong side)—With C, purl. (Join Color A.)
  Rows 2 and 4—With A, knit.

SQUARE 58: *Blister Stitch*

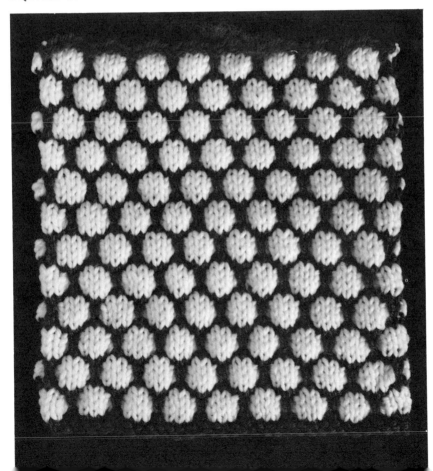

Rows 3 and 5—With A, purl.

Row 6—With C, k3, * drop next st off needle and unravel 4 rows down; insert right-hand needle from front into Color C st in 5th row below, and knit, catching the 4 loose strands in st; k3; rep from *.

Row 7—With C, purl.

Rows 8, 9, 10, and 11—Repeat Rows 2, 3, 4, and 5.

Row 12—With C, k1, rep from * of Row 6; end last repeat k1 instead of k3.

Repeat Rows 1–12 six times (72 rows). Bind off *loosely* on wrong side with C, purling all stitches.

This pattern teaches you not to be afraid of dropping stitches off the needle. Dropped stitches don't really unravel very well by themselves. They have to be helped. Help them not by pulling the knitting apart, but by gently plucking the Color A strands out of the dropped stitch one by one with the right-hand needle point. When you pick up the Color C stitch, below, be sure to insert the needle under all 4 A strands and catch them all securely in the stitch as you knit it.

Square 59: **Dip-Stitch Check**

Colors A and D. Techniques: k, p, dip
Multiple of 4 stitches plus 1

With A, cast on 37 stitches.

Row 1 (wrong side)—With A, purl.

Row 2—With A, knit.

Row 3—With A, purl. (Join D.)

Row 4—With D, * k3, dip needle point into front of the st in 3rd row below next st, draw a loose loop through, knit next st and pass dipped loop over the knit st; rep from *, end k1.

Rows 5, 6, and 7—With D, repeat Rows 1, 2, and 3.

Row 8—With A, k1, * dip into front of the st in 3rd row below next st, knit next st, pass dipped loop over as before; k3; rep from *.

Repeat Rows 1–8 six times, then Rows 1–5 again (53 rows). Bind off on right side with D, knitting all stitches.

SQUARE 59: *Dip-Stitch Check*

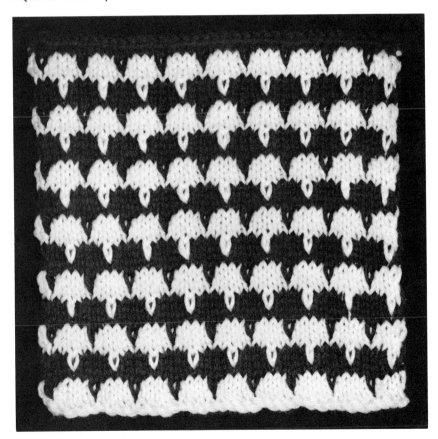

Dip Stitches are usually, but not always, either passed over or worked together with the next stitch on the needle. In other dip-stitch patterns, the extra loops are sometimes treated as increases. When working Dip Stitches, be sure to draw through long, loose loops so that the fabric will not be pinched by them.

Square 60: **Short-Row Stripes**

Colors A and C. Techniques: k, p, turn
Multiple of 14 stitches plus 1

With A, cast on 43 stitches. Purl one row. Join C.
   Row 1 (right side)—With C, knit.
   Row 2—With C, purl.
   Row 3—With A, knit.
   Row 4—With A, p12, * turn, k8, turn, p7, turn, k6, turn, p5, turn, k4, turn, p20; rep from *, end last repeat p9.
   Rows 5 and 6—With C, repeat Rows 1 and 2.
   Rows 7 and 8—With A, repeat Rows 1 and 2.
   Row 9—With C, knit.
   Row 10—With C, p5, turn, k5, turn, p4, turn, k4, turn, p19, * turn, k8, turn, p7, turn, k6, turn, p5, turn, k4, turn, p20; rep from *, end last repeat p16; then at end of row, turn, k5, turn, p5, turn, k4, turn, p4.
   Rows 11 and 12—With A, repeat Rows 1 and 2.

Repeat Rows 1–12 three times, then Rows 1–3 again (39 rows). Bind off on wrong side with A, purling all stitches.

Short rows are extremely useful in garment shaping. With the turns placed 4 or 5 stitches apart, for instance, they make the best way of

SQUARE 60: *Short-Row Stripes*

forming a shoulder slope. To prevent leaving a hole in the knitting whenever you work a short-row turn, do it like this: holding the yarn to the right side of the work, slip the *next unworked* stitch temporarily in order to pass the yarn around this stitch to the wrong side; then re-place the unworked stitch on its original needle and turn the work around.

Square 61: **Parquet Squares**

Colors A and D. Techniques: k, pick up
Multiple: any number of stitches

With A, cast on 21 stitches. Knit one row (this is the first wrong-side row). Join D.

Rows 1 and 2—With D, knit.
Rows 3 and 4—With A, knit.

SQUARE 61: *Parquet Squares*

Repeat these 4 rows until there are 21 2-row stripes, 10 stripes of Color D and 11 stripes of Color A counting the first wrong-side row. Break D. Bind off with A on right side, knitting all stitches. Keep last bound-off stitch on needle. Turn the square clockwise a quarter turn, so that the right side is facing and the left-hand edge uppermost. With A, pick up 20 stitches along this edge, one stitch from each stripe beginning with the first D stripe, to make a total of 21 stitches. Turn. Knit one row. Join D.

Repeat the same 4 rows until there are 21 stripes on the second square. As for first square, break D, bind off, turn the work one-quarter clockwise, and pick up 20 stitches for third square. Repeat the same process again for fourth square.

After picking up stitches for the fourth square, with right side still facing, * pick up *one more* stitch from the cast-on edge at the bottom of the first square. With left-hand needle, pass the second stitch on right-hand needle over the first stitch and off needle, thus eliminating the extra stitch. Repeat from * at the end of every right-side row throughout fourth square, to attach this side edge to the cast-on edge. Finish and bind off fourth square like the other three, drawing yarn through last bound-off stitch to fasten off.

Picking up stitches is a way of making a firm join, without sewing, between two pieces of knitting worked in different directions. It is used in garments to begin neckbands, borders, button bands and sometimes sleeves. It's important to know how to pick up stitches evenly and neatly, as almost every project in knitting involves a little of this technique somewhere.

Square 62: **Decreasing Seamless Square (Stockinette Stitch)**

Colors A and C. Techniques: k, sl 2—k1—p2sso
Multiple of 4 stitches

With 16″ circular needle and A, cast on 156 stitches. Join, first making sure that the stitches are not twisted on the needle. * Place a marker, k39; rep from * 3 times more. Join Color C. Slip first marker.

Round 1—With C, * knit to 3 sts before next marker, sl 2—k1—p2sso; remove marker, k1, replace marker; rep from * 3 times more.
Round 2—With C, knit, slipping each marker. Drop C on wrong side, pick up A.
Round 3—With A, repeat Round 1.
Round 4—With A, repeat Round 1. Drop A on wrong side, pick up C.
Rounds 5, 6, and 7—Repeat Rounds 1, 2, and 3.
Round 8—With A, repeat Round 2.

Repeat Rounds 1–8 until only 4 stitches remain. When stitches become too few to stretch around the 16″ circular needle, switch to a set of double-pointed needles and continue working around, using 3 needles to hold the stitches and the fourth needle for knitting. Helpful hint: to prevent looseness of stitches, always knit 2 or 3 stitches into the next needle before starting to use the free needle.

When 4 stitches remain, break yarn, leaving a 4″ tail. With a yarn needle, thread the yarn-end through the last 4 stitches. Fasten off on wrong side.

The Decreasing Seamless Square is a good design for mats, bags, pil-

(Opposite) SQUARE 62: *Decreasing Seamless Square*

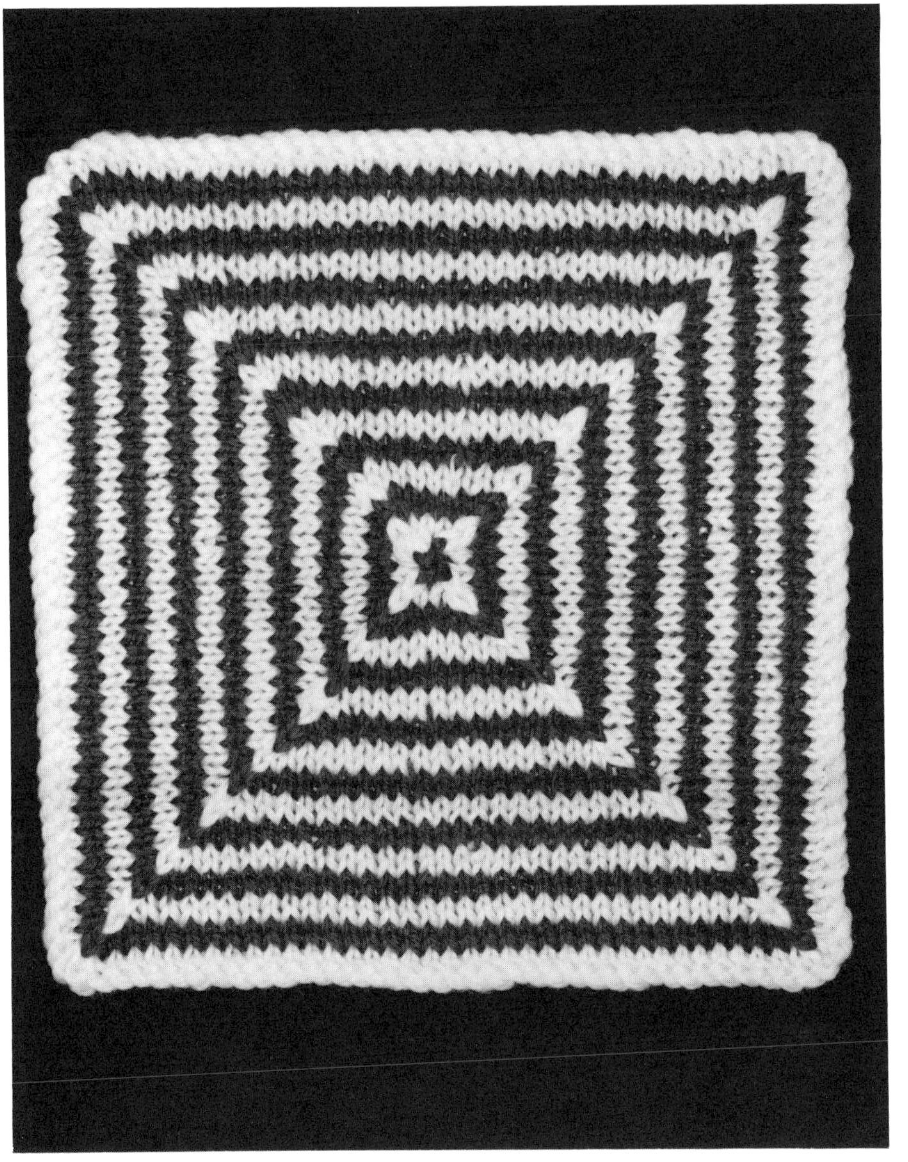

lows and potholders; it also illustrates the basic technique used in knitting a raglan yoke from the bottom up. Usually, for a seamless raglan yoke, the double decreases are made every other round. But in this case they are made on 5 rounds out of 8 (i.e., Rounds 1, 3, 4, 5, and 7) because a square of Stockinette Stitch will lie flatter when the double decreases are so spaced.

Notice that in circular knitting a Stockinette Stitch fabric is created by knitting every round. There is no purling. This applies equally to flat seamless pieces like this square, and to tubular pieces like seamless socks, sweaters and hats.

Square 63: **Increasing Seamless Square (Garter Stitch)**

Colors B and D. Techniques: k, p, inc, double inc
Multiple of 4 stitches

With one double-pointed needle and B, cast on 4 stitches. Knit one row, increasing in each of the 4 stitches to make 8 stitches. Divide these 8 stitches on 3 dp needles, being careful not to twist, and join them together. Join Color D. With D, knit one round, increasing in each of the 8 stitches to make 16 stitches. With D, * place a marker, p4; rep from * 3 times more. Drop D on wrong side, pick up B. With B, knit, slipping all markers.

Round 1—With B, * sl marker, double inc, purl to next marker; rep from * 3 times more. Drop B on wrong side, pick up D.
Round 2—With D, * remove marker, k1, replace marker, knit to next marker; rep from * 3 times more. Slip the last st of this round.
Round 3—With D, repeat Round 1. Drop D on wrong side, pick up B.
Round 4—With B, repeat Round 2.

Repeat Rounds 1–4, transferring the work from dp needles to the 16″ circular needle when there are more than 80 stitches. When there are 19 2-round stripes—9 D stripes and 10 B stripes counting the central cast-on rosette—break D, work Round 1 once more, and bind off with B, knitting all stitches.

The Increasing Seamless Square has the same uses as the Decreasing Seamless Square. Its obvious advantage is that its final size does not

SQUARE 63: *Increasing Seamless Square*

have to be planned in advance; the knitter can simply keep working round after round until the square has grown to the desired dimensions. This Garter Stitch version illustrates the basic technique for knitting a seamless raglan yoke from the neck down, with the customary rate of increasing 2 stitches at each corner every other round.

Notice that in circular knitting a Garter Stitch fabric is created by knitting one round and purling the next. This applies to any seamless circular knitting, flat or tubular. Like anything worked in Garter Stitch, this Seamless Square lies flat and requires little or no pressing.

BLOCKING, FINISHING AND JOINING

Use Square 1 as a model for blocking all your afghan squares. Lightly steam-press Square 1, then lay it on a piece of heavy fabric, like canvas, or your ironing-board cover, and mark the fabric around all edges. With thick contrasting thread, make a running-stitch in the fabric on the marks around this model square. Pin each of the other afghan squares one by one to the fabric, making sure that the edges lie exactly on your guidelines of thread, and steam-press.

Some pattern squares will require a little stretching to show their patterns—such as lace—to best advantage. Others should be allowed to shrink slightly into the model size to maintain a raised texture. Do not press hard on squares that have a raised texture, such as cables. Hold the weight of the iron up from the surface, so that it barely touches the knitting, and let the square adjust itself to correct shape under the steam. Naturally, the fabric, with its marked guide-square, must be kept stretched tight and flat; so it's a good idea to pin the fabric together .

underneath your ironing-board if you're not using the ironing-board cover itself.

When all squares have been blocked, lay them out on the floor and arrange your afghan. If you have used 4 colors according to the directions, you will have 6 different color combinations: A, B, A+C, A+D, B+C and B+D. You can arrange these combinations at random or else follow any system that pleases you. If you want to follow the system that was used in the sample afghan, it goes like this:

First (left-hand) column, top to bottom: BD, B, AC, A, BC, B, AD, A, BD.

Second column, top to bottom: A, BD, B, AC, A, BC, B, AD, A.

Third column, top to bottom: AD, A, BD, B, AC, A, BC, B, AD.

Fourth (center) column, top to bottom: B, AD, A, BD, B, AC, A, BC, B.

Fifth column, top to bottom: BC, B, AD, A, BD, B, AC, A, BC.

Sixth column, top to bottom: A, BC, B, AD, A, BD, B, AC, A.

Seventh (right-hand) column, top to bottom: AC, A, BC, B, AD, A, BD, B, AC.

Squares may be finished and joined together in any one of a number of different ways, as follows:

(1) Simple hand sewing. Thread a yarn needle with yarn and sew squares together from the right side. If you wish, you may overcast the edges first or else work around them with buttonhole or blanket stitch in contrasting yarn.

(2) Machine sewing. Overcast or buttonhole-stitched edges may be sewn together on a zigzag machine; or untreated edges may be basted together and covered with stretch seam binding or rug binding applied with machine sewing. It's best to place binding strips on both right and wrong sides of the afghan, covering all adjoining edges and binding around all outside edges. To apply binding, use plenty of pins and stretch as you sew, so the knitting will not be deformed in the process.

(3) Lining. To put an extra fabric backing on your afghan, it's most convenient to line each square separately. Cut 63 squares of lining fabric the same size as your model. Baste each knitted square to a lining square. Attach binding around all 4 edges. Sew the lined and bound squares together by hand or by machine.

(4) Crochet. Using a contrasting yarn and size H crochet hook, loosely work 1 row of single crochet all the way around each square, placing about 20 sc along each side and 3 sc in each corner. Crochet-bordered squares then may be crocheted together, or sewn together with a simple overcast stitch. Work an extra row or two of single crochet all the way around outside edges of the finished afghan, increasing at corners.

(5) Seamless knitted borders. Using a circular needle or a set of double-pointed needles and contrasting yarn, pick up border stitches all the way around each square, 39 stitches from each side and 1 stitch from each corner. Purl the first round, knit the next round, purl the next, knit the next, and so on, to make a border of Garter Stitch; work a double increase in each corner every other round, as in Square 63. When the border is as wide as you wish it, bind off all the way around. Knit-bordered squares then may be sewn or woven together. Outside edges require no extra finishing unless you want to add an edging or fringe.

To make fringe for an afghan put together with hand-sewing, crocheting or knitting, wind contrasting yarn many times around a piece of cardboard as wide as the desired length of fringe strands. Cut through all strands in one place. Knot each fringe strand by its center into the afghan edge. The quickest and simplest way to do this is to double each strand and insert the loop into the eye of a yarn needle; draw the loop through the afghan edge, remove the yarn needle, then pass both free ends through the loop and pull tight. The more fringe strands you use, the thicker the fringe. For a fancier fringe, separate adjoining strands or groups of strands and knot them to their neighbors along the edge.

Of course there are possible variations on all methods of finishing and joining, and if you prefer to do something different from the foregoing descriptions, then by all means do it your own way. After all, it's your afghan. Enjoy it and be proud of it; and think of it as a kind of welcome-mat leading you into the ranks of accomplished knitters.